LIBERAL CONSTITUTIONALISM, MARRIAGE, AND SEXUAL ORIENTATION

TEACHING TEXTS IN LAW AND POLITICS

David A. Schultz
General Editor

Vol. 15

PETER LANG
New York • Washington, D.C./Baltimore • Bern
Frankfurt am Main • Berlin • Brussels • Vienna • Oxford

Gordon Albert Babst

LIBERAL CONSTITUTIONALISM, MARRIAGE, AND SEXUAL ORIENTATION

A Contemporary Case for Dis-Establishment

PETER LANG
New York • Washington, D.C./Baltimore • Bern
Frankfurt am Main • Berlin • Brussels • Vienna • Oxford

Library of Congress Cataloging-in-Publication Data
Babst, Gordon Albert.
Liberal constitutionalism, marriage, and sexual orientation:
a contemporary case for dis-establishment / Gordon Albert Babst.
p. cm. — (Teaching texts in law and politics; v. 15)
Includes bibliographical references and index.
1. Same-sex marriage—Law and legislation—United States.
2. Gays—Legal status, laws, etc.—United States. 3. Marriage law—
United States. 4. Religion and law—United States.
5. Constitutional law—Religious aspects. I. Title. II. Series.
KF539 .B33 346.7301'6—dc21 2002067546
ISBN 0-8204-5533-4
ISSN 1083-3447

Die Deutsche Bibliothek-CIP-Einheitsaufnahme
Babst, Gordon Albert:
Liberal constitutionalism, marriage, and sexual orientation:
a contemporary case for dis-establishment / Gordon Albert Babst.
−New York; Washington, D.C./Baltimore; Bern;
Frankfurt am Main; Berlin; Brussels; Vienna; Oxford: Lang.
(Teaching texts in law and politics; Vol. 15)
ISBN 0-8204-5533-4

Cover design by Lisa Barfield

The paper in this book meets the guidelines for permanence and durability
of the Committee on Production Guidelines for Book Longevity
of the Council of Library Resources.

© 2002 Peter Lang Publishing, Inc., New York
275 Seventh Avenue, 28th Floor, New York, NY 10001
www.peterlangusa.com

All rights reserved.
Reprint or reproduction, even partially, in all forms such as microfilm,
xerography, microfiche, microcard, and offset strictly prohibited.

Printed in the United States of America

To the memory of Dante Germino (1931–2002).

Dante Germino, who passed away tragically on May 25, 2002, was an eminent political philosopher and close friend.

Contents

Preface ix

Introduction 1
Organization of the Book 5
Six Features of Contemporary Public Law 6

Part I
Marriage in the Law 11

Chapter One. Marriage as Contract and Status 15

Chapter Two. The Defense of Marriage Act and Recent Events in State Law 22

Part II
The Law and Morality Distinction, Violated 35

Chapter Three. Morals Discourse and Law 41

Chapter Four. Professor Richards Finds a Violation 51

Part III
How to Identify Sub Rosa Establishment and the Argument by Definition 61

Chapter Five. The Shadow Establishment Has Its Day in Court 67

Chapter Six. A Note Regarding the Appeal to the Dictionary 80

Part IV
The *Shadow Establishment*, "Gay Marriage" in the Courts, and the Analogies to Race and Polygamy 85

Chapter Seven. Interracial and Plural Marriage Analogies and Cases 91
The Miscegenation Analogy 91
The Polygamy Analogy 95

Chapter Eight. "Gay Marriage" in the Courts 100

Conclusion 107

Table of Cases 113

Notes 115

Bibliography 143

Index 153

Preface

Liberal Constitutionalism, Marriage, and Sexual Orientation: A Contemporary Case for Dis-Establishment, uses constitutional theory and political philosophy to shed light on an elusive feature of American jurisprudence: the establishment of a sectarian preference in the law to the detriment of American citizens who happen to be gay or lesbian, and who wish to exercise their fundamental right to marry. This preference is uncovered through a broad-ranging examination of the rationale for the ban on same-sex marriage. Since marriage is considered a fundamental interest, an aspect of personal liberty, equal protection of the law should guarantee this right to all Americans, and allow each adult individual to marry the person of his or her choice. We argue that the State has no genuine interest compelling enough to override this fundamental liberty interest, but that it, instead, believes itself to be protecting what is substantially a religious value, the good of marriage.

Reviewing aspects of liberal-democratic theory, marriage law, and pertinent analogies that deal with the right to marry, we present the notion of the *shadow establishment* as that which makes the best sense of a constitutional affirmation of bias against same-sex marriage and also gay persons in the law. The freedom from religious establishment of some American citizens is violated by this *shadow establishment* of a generalized, widely-shared but nonetheless sectarian perspective regarding the institution of marriage. The *de jure* ban on same-sex marriage is, therefore, constitutionally suspect. The *shadow establishment*, a non-preferentialist sectarian bias, is revealed through discussions that include the no religious test clause, Sunday closing laws, and marriage law as it has related to mixed-race couples, Mormons, and gay or lesbian American citizens.

Supporters of the ban on same-sex marriage are cast as out-of-step with the nature of the American political regime, because they are opposed not merely to the full legal recognition of same-sex couples' right to marry, an exercise of any American citizen's fundamental liberty interest, but also to the public liberal-democratic values of our constitutionally ordered republic.

Introduction

~

For the cases present the ordinances in actual operation, and the facts shown establish an administration directed so exclusively against a particular class of persons as to warrant and require the conclusion that whatever may have been the intent of the ordinances as adopted, they are applied by the public authorities charged with their administration, and thus representing the State itself, with a mind so unequal and oppressive as to amount to a practical denial by the State of that equal protection of the laws which is secured to the petitioners, as to all other persons, by the broad and benign provisions of the Fourteenth Amendment to the Constitution of the United States. Though the law itself be fair on its face and impartial in appearance, yet, if it is applied and administered by public authority with an evil eye and an unequal hand, so as practically to make unjust and illegal discriminations between persons in similar circumstances, material to their rights, the denial of equal justice is still within the prohibition of the Constitution.[1]

The argument of this book is that the notion of a continuing *shadow establishment* of religion in the United States today provides a very good explanation for the ongoing legal ban on same-sex marriage. This ban allows some Americans to maintain marriage as a legally frozen institution, and to keep gay persons, one to another, legal strangers in the eyes of the law. By "explanation," we mean to identify what gives the ban its core sense of "right," "good," or "reasonable" that its legality or constitutionality is taken suitably to protect. Religion is meant broadly, not to denote a full-blown institutionalization in the law of the tenets of a particular faith, but the presence of religious rather than secular persuasion. Furthermore, this religious persuasion is identifiable within a

Judeo-Christian framework, rather than a generalized expression of any alternative faith, much in keeping with the nation's religious heritage. For our purposes it is not necessary to hazard a guess as to whether certain justices or legislators intend their decisions and lines of argument to be read as religious in nature, when they are not explicit about this aspect. An alternative explanation to that developed here is to assert that there simply is no underlying, cohesive, identifiable rationale or perspective to account for the soundness of the ban on same-sex marriage, or the good its supporters believe they are accomplishing; it just makes good public policy sense. One philosopher and legal scholar renders this sense of attributing a point-of-view as follows:

> These [religious] views are attributed to the Court not because the Court states them, but primarily because attributing them to the Court helps make sense of what the Court has stated and decided, much as attributing gravitational attraction to physical mass helps makes sense of lunar movements and tidal changes.[2]

The spirit of the laws here are best regarded as religious in nature or rationale, resulting in a *de jure* ban on same-sex marriage.

We suggest that this ban can best be made sense of in the light of the notion of the *shadow establishment*, which we identify as *an impermissible expression of sectarian preference in the law that is unreasonable in the light of the nation's constitutional commitments to all its citizens*. We understand *sectarian* to mean resting on perceptions internal to religious convictions, as opposed to a public justification that uses arguments accessible to all citizens and consistent with the United States Constitution. It is generally the case that people understand "sectarian" and "secular" as paired opposites, but these terms are better understood politically by their contrast with "public." Secular may indeed mean a comprehensive moral vision, just one that is not religious in nature. Public implies no adherence to a comprehensive moral doctrine of any kind, though in the United States it implies adherence to liberal-democratic values and principles such as characterize the American constitutional republic. Herein, whenever the term "secular" is used, it is not to imply any comprehensive moral doctrine, but as a shorthand for "public" and to emphasize its not being sectarian or religious.[3] It is our view that no existing sectarian or secular comprehensive moral vision or doctrine by itself supplies political reasons for public policy or law in the American context. Nevertheless, religion has been a prominent political issue in the nation's history, one especially contentious in those instances where this or that aspect of the

American citizenry has been legally estranged on a religious basis. In those instances, the dispute is clarified by understanding it not as about morality, but about political power and control of the political process. The notion of the *shadow establishment* clarifies when one party to the dispute, that side whose view of public law is overdetermined by religion, runs afoul of the Constitution.

In making the argument this essay surveys several representative lines of reasoning found in court decisions and scholarly discussions, and focuses attention on the First and Fourteenth Amendments to the U.S. Constitution, as well as the "no religious test" clause of Article VI. The latter is often forgotten by scholars when treating the relationship between church and state:

> Among the mountains of literature on church and state, only a handful of book chapters and articles focus on the Article VI, clause 3 prohibition. Indeed, the attention given the First Amendment has been so complete that one could be forgiven for concluding that the federal religious test ban was of little historical or substantive significance to the constitutional framework for church-state relations. It is curious. . . . The test ban was thus calculated to secure religious liberty, deter religious persecution, ensure sect equality before the law, and promote institutional independence of civil government from ecclesiastical domination and interference at the federal level. . . . It was among the truly innovative features of the American Constitution. . . . With uncommon boldness, the constitutional framers proposed a clause deliberately calculated to ensure sect equality before the law and promote institutional independence of civil government from ecclesiastical domination at the federal level.[4]

We use constitutional theory and political philosophy to shed light on an elusive feature of American jurisprudence: the establishment of sectarian preference for religion in the law. This preference is uncovered through a broad-ranging examination of the rationale for the ban on same-sex marriage, which, we will discover, is not coequal with a ban on "gay marriage," forms of which are recognized in the law.[5]

Since marriage is considered a fundamental right, equal protection of the law should guarantee this taken-for-granted liberty interest to all Americans, and allow each adult individual to marry the person of his or her choice. We argue that the State has no genuine interest compelling enough to override this fundamental liberty interest, but that it, instead, believes itself to be protecting what is substantially a religious value, a sectarian understanding of the good of marriage, the constitutional weight of which merits serious challenge. Not to appreciate the nature of the rationale supporting the ban, is not to understand it, because no public policy considerations can provide the muscle necessary to overcome the liberty interest at stake—that of an adult to marry the loved one of her choice, not the liberty interest in maintaining the exclusivity of a sectarian heteronormative understanding of the marital relationship.

Reviewing aspects of liberal-democratic theory, marriage law, and pertinent analogies that deal with the right to marry, we present the notion of the *shadow establishment* as that which makes the best sense of a constitutional affirmation of bias against same-sex marriage in the law. The freedom from religious establishment of some American citizens is violated by this *shadow establishment* of a generalized, widely shared but nonetheless sectarian perspective regarding the institution of marriage. The injurious nature of the ban as well as its animating rationale, however, are not invisible to those who strive to understand it and who seek a statement of public justification for it. The *de jure* ban on same-sex marriage is, therefore, constitutionally suspect, as argued in the following chapters that seek out and make explicit this sectarian preference in Sunday closing laws and marriage law as it has related to mixed-race couples, Mormons, and American citizens who happen to be gay or lesbian.

Denying to American gay men and lesbians the considerable legal rights and benefits government bestows on married spouses merits studied consideration, especially given that these provisions are intended to encourage couples to marry.[6] Society's gradual unmooring of marriage from religious conceptions and from "heteronormativity," a term we discuss later, suggests a disconnect between the current state of the law and the American society it serves. The law's usefulness as a bar to a particular variety of potentially unjust discrimination has not been fully exploited until the nature of this disconnect is revealed, and an appropriate legal response crafted. In other contexts besides the issue at hand here, many people of goodwill find the effects of sexual orientation discrimination, no matter its precise genealogy, to be odious and un-American.

The argument presented here is not an argument "for" gay marriage; however, it is a disestablishment argument.[7] We neither recommend nor discourage individual same-sex couples, gay or otherwise, to enter into a same-sex marriage, nor do we comment on the desirability of the institution of marriage for any couple.[8] The controversy over the same-sex marriage question may provide Americans with an opportunity to reevaluate their social preferences for certain family formations, especially those ensconced in the law. Today the scaffold of legitimate state interests surrounding the marriage ban are at sea, and the structure as such is at issue. Contemporary scholars are revealing a picture of marriage as having had many aims, which have proved mutable in both form and significance.[9] Indeed, the "purpose" of the marital relationship is being revealed as not self-evident, or at least not so obvious that denial of entry into it is automatic or just.[10]

Organization of the Book

In addition to the brief overview of the book already provided, the Introduction presents and discusses some public policy considerations that have been advanced in argument to suggest the legitimacy of the ban on same-sex marriage. In Part I we present the legal understanding of marriage (Chapter One), and review recent events in the law at the state level, as well as the Defense of Marriage Act or DOMA (Chapter Two). Part II presents and reviews some pertinent literature on morals discourse and law, and argues for the proposition that heterosexuality is not merely a sexual concept, but largely a normative one, imbued with religious significance (Chapter Three). We then focus attention on a unique law review essay that treats sexual orientation discrimination as unconstitutional under the religion clauses of the First Amendment (Chapter Four).[11] In Part III we denote how to identify *sub rosa* religious establishment, or *shadow establishment,* through the Supreme Court's reasoning in some key First Amendment/Establishment cases, where several members of the Court very ably exhumed the impermissible entanglement of church and state in the areas of Sunday closing laws and time set-asides for religious instruction in the public schools (Chapter Five). We next present and deconstruct the argument against same-sex marriage based on the purported definition of marriage (Chapter Six). Part IV presents the analogies arguably relevant to the *de jure* ban on same-sex marriage. These analogies are taken from cases involving miscegenation and Mormon polygamy, which, we argue, explicitly implicate a sectarian preference in the law (Chapter Seven). Finally, we review the issue of same-sex marriage in the courts, as well as draw and interrogate the distinction between same-sex marriage and "gay marriage" (Chapter Eight). The Conclusion reiterates the thesis that the ban on same-sex marriage is grounded in the continuing *shadow establishment* of religion in the United States today, and so is constitutionally infirm for want of legitimate public justification.

Six Features of Contemporary Public Law

Over the course of the last decade some public policy considerations have been advanced in argument to suggest the legitimacy of the legal ban on same-sex marriage. Below we present and discuss six public policy features of the law, some or all of which currently are present in several jurisdictions below the federal level. These features respond to the most frequently cited public policy bars to the legal recognition of same-sex unions; arguably exhaust the state's secular interest in maintaining the ban; and also provide the context for the argument of the entire book. In addition, as one would expect of public policy, these features are subject to open, empirical investigation.[12] Neither a secular argument, nor, of course, a sectarian argument, can carry the burden of legitimating the ban on same-sex marriage in the law, absent some legitimate and express public purpose, such as is incorporated in each of the six considerations that follow.

Feature # 1

No anti-sodomy statute is in effect, thus ruling out this sort of criminal sanction as a bar to same-sex marriage, as is the case in thirty-six states and in the District of Columbia.[13] Sodomy laws have affected the legal status of gay persons even in those states which have removed them, because they create a presumption of criminal behavior that may inhibit their ability not only to marry, but also to change residence and jobs.[14] As of July, 2001, only fourteen states continue to provide criminal penalties for sodomy in private and between consenting adults. In eleven of these states the antisodomy statute is directed at both same-sex and heterosexual practices, with the remaining three (Kansas, Oklahoma, Texas) criminalizing only homosexual sodomy.[15] Not all antisodomy statutes could be constructed to bar same-sex marriage in any case.

For example, Georgia Code Annotated Section 16-6-2 (1984), famously upheld by the Supreme Court in *Bowers v. Hardwick* (478 U.S. 186 [1986]), provided as follows:

> (a) A person commits the offense of sodomy when he performs or submits to any sexual act involving the sex organs of one person and the mouth or anus of another. A person commits the offense of aggravated sodomy when he commits sodomy with force and against the will of the other person.
>
> (b) A person convicted of the offense of sodomy shall be punished by imprisonment for not less than one nor more than 20 years. A person convicted of

the offense of aggravated sodomy shall be punished by imprisonment for life or by not less than one nor more than 20 years.[16]

Note that this statute is facially neutral as regards the participants' sexual orientation, gender, and marriage status. This case has elicited innumerable response from the academic community.[17] Despite the neutrality of many anti-sodomy statutes, "there is apparently no reported judicial opinion in which a heterosexual has been denied custody, visitation, or other parental right based on a sodomy statute . . . despite the fact that . . . most heterosexuals violate them."[18] To the extent that sodomy laws bolster and support the ban, they have the effect of reducing marriage to sexual intimacy, and of conflating that with a certain physical act, reductions in the laudable stature of marriage its supporters ought to find discomfiting.

Given that as recently as 1960 all fifty states and the District of Columbia outlawed consensual sodomy in one form or another, this has been a sea change in the law that once served to brand gay and lesbian Americans as *de facto* criminals, as second-class citizens, fusing their identity and the conduct that purportedly best identifies them. The effects of sodomy laws reverberate far beyond their rare actual enforcement against parties to a particular sex act, and across state lines where respect is accorded them under the full faith and credit clause, ultimately to "achieve indirectly what the states cannot do directly: criminalize homosexuals."[19]

Feature # 2

An anti-discrimination ordinance is in place, banning discrimination on the basis of sexual orientation, thus indicating legislative will not to have the law treat gay and lesbian persons differently from heterosexual persons, or to treat the former with the same fairness as the latter. In the United States today, twenty states and the District of Columbia have a gay rights ordinance on the books banning the following specific kinds of discrimination based in sexual orientation: public employment (twenty States and DC); public accommodations (eleven states and DC); private employment (thirteen states and DC); education (seven states and DC); housing (nine states and DC); credit (seven states); and, union practices (nine states and DC).[20]

In those jurisdictions with gay rights statutes on the books, one cannot blithely assume that gay persons are moral outcasts warranting differential treatment in the law to reflect the community's bias against them, or in favor of one or other way of life. Such statutes suggest a contrary state of affairs, one that does not turn on sexual orientation. Though these advances in the law should not be taken to indicate an emerging consensus as regards relationships between gay persons, they may well indicate an invigorated commitment to fairness and equal protection of the laws toward individual persons who are similarly situated and traditionally prone to discriminatory treatment by virtue of their minority sexual orientation.

The legal grounds and protections offered through anti-discrimination laws, and the accordance of rights and responsibilities in so-called "gay rights" statutes have been taken to indicate a political group that has arrived and seized power. Therefore, this line of reasoning continues, gays and lesbians need no longer be considered a politically disempowered constituency in American society.[21] Repeal efforts directed against gay rights measures across the United States suggest that this line of reasoning is inaccurate. During oral argument before the Court in *Romer v. Evans* (116 S.Ct. 1620 [1996]), several justices expressed puzzlement as to what was "special" about rights such as mentioned above, which can be presumed by every citizen, yet which supporters of a recently passed, statewide anti-gay initiative would reverse, and as to what the purpose of the initiative was, except to be adopted for its own sake as an expression of majoritarian sentiment.[22]

Feature # 3

The allowance for same-sex couples to adopt children, thus eliminating the often-heard complaint that the presence of homosexual-oriented persons endangers children. The notion that gay persons are an inherent menace to children is rubbish and not in any way supported by social science evidence or analysis.[23] Of course, condemnation of gay and lesbian parents may never have benefitted from empirical warrant, being instead an instance of pure status discrimination against them as individuals.[24] A parent's sexual orientation has little bearing on the sexual orientation of his or her child.[25] Adoption by gay persons individually, or by same-sex couples, is either expressly permitted or is the common practice in twelve states and in the District of Columbia, and over "three million gay men and lesbians were raising between eight and ten million children in the United States" as early as 1987.[26]

Feature # 4

Legal custody rights for gay and lesbian biological parents—thus another validation of these persons' worthiness as parents and right to maintain their families.[27] Those states that recognize gay and lesbian families suggest that they perceive no distinction between them and traditional heterosexual families, at least at the level of fundamentals, which do not map out by sexual orientation.[28] Indeed, there are and always have been a variety of functioning family forms, with some burdened where others are affirmed. As a recent study of norms of the family today has put it:

> On the one hand, unconventional families are accused of threatening the values and commitments for which families stand. On the other hand, when they attempt to demonstrate those very same commitments and values, they are denied the opportunity to incorporate them into their lives. . . . The modern family is, in fact, a number of different families.[29]

Feature # 5

Domestic partner registration possibilities, whereby same-sex couples can register their ongoing, stable unions with a governing body, thus indicating legislative intent to confer worth, rather than condemnation on these relationships.[30] Three states and the District of Columbia provide domestic partner registry listings.[31] As of July, 2001, seven states, the District of Columbia, and over 50 cities and counties offered domestic partner benefits to their government employees, indicating a legislative affirmation, rather than neglect, of the standing of gay persons' relationships.[32] The recent Census 2000 revealed a mix of family structures in the United States with a significant number of "nonfamily households," with about 6.5 million householders living with other unrelated individuals, about six percent of all occupied households.[33]

Feature # 6

An "equal rights amendment" in place, thus forbidding the state from defending its bar(s) to same-sex marriage on the basis of traditional male and female roles. Provisions in states' equal rights amendments are mindful of the fact that although ordinarily gender norms are unwritten, they nonetheless produce standardized behaviors the violation of which brings sanctions that the law must frequently be scrutinized for imposing, should they consist of impermissible definitions or limitations.[34] Gay men have long been thought to violate gender norms, to "act like women."[35] On May 5, 1993, however, the Supreme Court of Hawaii vacated and remanded for further consideration the State of Hawaii's recently enacted statute banning same-sex marriage by applying the strict scrutiny standard of review as warranted under the section of the Hawaii Constitution prohibiting state-sanctioned discrimination on the basis of sex.[36] There should be no legal distinction between treating the gay man as a "man" or as a "woman," and any gender specificity in the law should not obscure the Constitution's commitment to equal citizenship.

∽

With the above features, and possibly others as well legally in place, the task of making the ban on same-sex marriage understandable is all the more pressing.[37] Put differently, ruling out the above given policy considerations, which conceivably exhaust all express purposes of legitimate interest to the state, how can we explain the ban? Absent these features, what is the minimally rational basis for the ban that voids the charge that it is an arbitrary and so unconstitutional abridgment of liberty?[38] The question becomes irrepressible: Why not allow gay and lesbian couples to marry, and grant to them equal legal recognition?

Part I reviews traditional marriage law, and recent events in the states as well as the Defense of Marriage Act. The purpose of Part I is to identify the spirit of the law here, by which is meant the rationale that makes sense of the law, possibly even in the face of the features given above. In subsequent chapters we will uncover and coax the *shadow establishment* out from under secular public purpose in the law, frequently with the assistance of some supporters of the ban on same-sex marriage who are unabashed about the sectarian nature of their claims for it. The ban and its supporters will be revealed not only successfully to have legislated their non-preferentialist sectarian preference, but also to be out-of-step with the nature of the American political regime, and marching instead to a different beat, one inconsistent with the American constitutional order.

PART I

Marriage in the Law

Most Americans regard their closest interpersonal relationships as among the most valuable aspects of a good life, well within their proper sphere of decision-making, and view any outside intrusions and state intervention as illegitimate. Many Americans may not be aware of cases such as **Loving v. Virginia** *(388 U.S. 1 [1967])*, where an interracial couple appealed to the Supreme Court to have their marriage validated, because they may naively believe that affairs of the heart are too impenetrable, and statute law ineffective to change our deepest feelings, such as we hold for the persons we love. Yet, the reality of American history regarding close interpersonal relationships belies this romantic view of adult citizens forming relations of affection undisturbed by the state. Below we quote from the most enduring, definitive statement the Court has given regarding marriage. In **Maynard v. Hill** *(31 L.Ed. 654 [1888])*, the Court validated the reigning understanding of marriage, an understanding that resonates to this day; as such, it is usefully quoted from at length.

> Marriage, as creating the most important relation in life, as having more to do with the morals and civilization of a people than any other institution, has always been subject to the control of the Legislature. . . . It is also to be observed that, whilst marriage is often termed by text writers and in decisions of courts as a civil contract—generally to indicate that it must be founded upon the agreement of the parties, and does not require any religious solemnization—it is something more than a mere contract. . . . Other contracts may be modified, restricted, or enlarged, or entirely released upon the consent of the parties. Not so with marriage. . . . It is an institution, in the maintenance of which in its purity the public is deeply interested, for it is the foundation of the family and of society, without which there would be neither civilization nor progress. . . . In strictness, though formed by contract, it signifies the relation of husband and wife, deriving both its rights and duties from a source higher than any contract of which the parties are

capable. . . . It is declared a civil contract for certain purposes, but it is not thereby made synonymous with the word contract employed in the common law or statutes. . . . The relation is always regulated by government. It is more than a contract. . . . Other distinctive elements will readily suggest themselves, which rob it of most of its characteristics as a contract, and leave it simply as a status or institution. As such, it is not so much the result of private agreement, as of public ordination. . . . It is a great public institution, giving character to our whole civil polity.[1]

The important elements of the traditional legal understanding of marriage, and of the nature of this most important of social relationships, were given in **Maynard**. There the Court linked marriage to "civilization" and "progress," a "higher source," "contract" and "status." The Court also recognized a state interest in marriage in its "purity" as the "foundation of the family and of society," and its being "subject to the control of the Legislature." Notwithstanding the theological tenor and overreach to universalism implied in Maynard, this understanding of marriage nevertheless constituted but one of several possible understandings, even at the time.[2] Nevertheless, the framework established in Maynard has endured, in all likelihood ensconcing a sectarian morals discourse in the law.

The law, of course, cannot have as its purpose to uphold the sacra mentality of marriage, for example, as a faith-strengthening relationship, because then religious conviction alone would give it its reason for being, which is unallowable in the American context. The next chapter presents the legal understanding of marriage as simultaneously civil contract and status. Bereft of sufficiently weighty secular public purpose(s), assuming arguendo that any at all are present in the ban, both it and the legislative acts discussed in Chapter Two stand revealed to lack legitimacy, given the fundamentality of the right and liberty interest at issue, as well as the potent, lurking suspicion that certain unpopular Americans are being sacrificed at the altar of a majority's received customs and sincerely-held convictions.

ONE

Marriage as Contract and Status

Marriage has evolved into a fundamental right; discrimination here is likely invidious. The freedom to marry is embraced under the liberty secured by the Due Process Clause of the Fourteenth Amendment, as well as its Equal Protection Clause. Marriage was given a comprehensive interpretation in *Zablocki v. Redhail* (434 U.S. 374 [1978]), where it was determined to be a fundamental liberty interest falling under the due process and equal protection clauses of the Fourteenth Amendment. *Zablocki* reaffirmed the fundamental character of the right to marry, even for people who had outstanding child support obligations from a previous marriage. Kenneth Karst has identified the issue presented to the Court in *Zablocki* as "what the right to marry implies. . . . Properly understood, *Zablocki* implies a thoroughgoing reassessment of the constitutionality of a wide range of state laws limiting the right to marry and restricting other nonmarital forms of intimate association."[1]

    Zablocki followed in a relatively fast train of mostly privacy cases that sorted out state laws regarding the right to marry, marriage laws, unmarried cohabitation, intimate relations within marriage, and heterosexual sexual relations outside of marriage. This train of cases brought in the federal government, on behalf of the individual, to challenge state laws and customs regulating marriage. Identification of the marital relationship as an individual's fundamental right with constitutional protection was recognized in the legal community shortly after *Griswold v. Connecticut* (381 U.S. 479 [1965]), affirming that marriage is a right of privacy older than the Bill of Rights, one in which private decisions such as whether to use contraception are protected, and the *Loving* case, which held that a state's regulation of marriage cannot contravene Constitutional guarantees to all American citizens, here proscribing racial discrimination in the selection of a spouse.[2]

In *Skinner v. State of Oklahoma* (316 U.S. 535 [1942]), the Court dealt with the forced sterilization of some convicts in the context of their rights to marriage and procreation. Here, the Court was concerned with "a feature of the Act which clearly condemns it," with "invidious discriminations. . . . When the law lays an unequal hand" on certain persons, depriving them of "one of the basic civil rights of man. Marriage and procreation are fundamental to the very existence and survival of the race."[3] In *Cleveland Board of Education v. LaFleur* (414 U.S. 632 [1974]), where a pregnant school teacher was discriminated against, the Court "recognized that freedom of choice in matters of marriage and family life is one of the liberties protected by the Due Process Clause of the Fourteenth Amendment."[4]

Marriage is a matter left to each state to regulate, within constitutional limits. Marriage is not mentioned in the U.S. Constitution, and so its regulation by the states falls within the ambit of the Tenth Amendment, which also reserves undelegated powers "to the people," by which ultimately is meant each and every citizen. Federal limitations on a state's regulation of the right to marry have been reaffirmed, following *Zablocki*:

> A state may deny the right to marry only for compelling reasons. . . . The right to marry is a fundamental right protected by the U.S. Constitution. . . . When the right to marry is involved, a regulation significantly interferes with exercise of the right when it directly and substantially interferes with the decision to marry or not to marry. . . . This is not to say there could never be a valid regulation of prisoner marriage based on enabling legislation reflecting a compelling state interest.[5]

State statutes on marriage identify it as a civil contract. This is frequently given in the opening lines of the marriage section of a state's family law statutes, such as in the following state statutes from Missouri and New York:

> Marriage is considered in law as a civil contract, to which the consent of the parties capable in law of contracting is essential.[6]

> Marriage, so far as its validity in law is concerned, continues to be a civil contract, to which the consent of the parties capable in law of making a contract is essential.[7]

Marriage is a *civil* contract because it denotes a legal relationship subject to the control of the secular state, rather than a couple's being legally bound as per one or other ecclesiastical authority, as in the following statute from California:

No contract of marriage, if otherwise duly made, shall be invalidated for want of conformity to the requirements of any religious sect.[8]

The state will recognize marriages solemnized by acceptable religious authorities, as well as by the state's agent(s), usually a justice of the peace, as in the following statutes from New Hampshire and Maryland:

> Marriage may be solemnized by a justice of the peace as comissioned in the state; by any minister of the gospel in the state who has been ordained according to the usage of his denomination, resides in the state, and is in regular standing with the denomination; by any clergyman who is not ordained but is engaged in the service of the religious body to which he belongs, resides in the state, after being licensed therefor by the secretary of state; and within his parish, by any minister residing out of the state, but having a pastoral charge wholly or partly in this state.[9]

> a) *Authorized officials.* A marriage may be performed in this State by:
>   (1) any official of a religious order or body authorized by the rules and customs of that order or body to perform a marriage ceremony;
>   (2 any clerk; or
>   (3) any deputy clerk designated by the county administrative judge of the circuit court for the county.[10]

That states recognize marriages performed by persons other than the clergy, when per the couple's request, discounts any notion of an exclusive role for religion in the solemnizing of a marriage, or in determining the couple's choice of solemnizing agent. This does not, however, speak to the notion or meaning of marriage in the minds of any authorized official, public or otherwise. This may well be an instance of collusion, where both religious and non-religious agents understand themselves to be doing the same thing, invoking the state's authority to solemnize or sanctify a matrimonial union just the same. Religious officials, for their part, seem not to object to the use of their services to further a state aim, one entirely secular when performed by an authorized public official.

Marriage is a civil *contract* because this relationship is consented to by the two individuals party to it, whose personal, voluntary decision to marry has a requisite effect upon recognition of the public commitment and license by the state, as in the following statutes from South Dakota and Georgia:

> Marriage is a personal relation arising out of a civil contract to which the consent of the parties capable of making it is necessary. Consent alone will not constitute a marriage; it must be followed by a solemnization.[11]

> To constitute an actual contract of marriage, the parties must consent thereto voluntarily without any fraud practiced upon either.... The policy of the law being opposed to restrictions on marriage and to marriages not the result of free choice, all contracts or bonds to hinder or to force marriage are deemed fraudulent and void.[12]

The marriage contract, however, creates a civil *status,* the unique status of being married. As with any other status, it cannot be discarded at will, but requires in this case legal dissolution. In this sense, the sense in which marriage is a status, being married is entering into a permanent relationship that is the particular couple's part of an ongoing, traditional institution. Scholars who have recently made marriage the object of their inquiries, have found that the ongoing, traditional institution of marriage has weathered the centuries because it has been adapted to the social, political, economic, legal, and religious turns of history, both shaping relationships and being shaped by them.[13]

The libertarian may well wonder what business it is of government to advance or retard the evolution of this institution, as theorist David Boaz argues:

> Why should government issue marriage licenses? A marriage is a voluntary agreement, a contract, which for many people has a deep religious meaning. What does it have to do with government? We should return to the notion of marriage as a civil contract for everyone and a religious covenant for those who choose it. Such a policy might even strengthen marriage. ... Couples should be allowed to write their own contracts, and courts should grant them the same respect that commercial contracts receive.[14]

The libertarian argument is that the state ought not concern itself with the identities of the adult individuals who choose to enter into a marriage relationship, or with whatever purposes they might have. The decision in *Zablocki* arguably comports well with a libertarian perspective: "equality of access to marriage, through the lens of individual choice," where the "choice is that of the individual, not the state. The state must justify any classification that significantly interferes with equality of access to marriage."[15]

Although marriage is not an ascribed status by dint of birth, it is a state-conferred legal status, which is entered into by contract and possibly affirmed by an authority in one or other religious tradition. The status of being married is performative; it is what the couple is and what they do together.[16] But the repertoire of possible performances continues to be gravely limited to heterosexual couples, and prohibited to same-sex couples, just as it once was to racially mixed couples and remains for plural marriages.[17] In the context of the American regime of equal citizenship, this limitation falls on individuals in the first instance, denying their access to an important status, a situation that domestic partnership legislation does not rectify. The argument that a lesbian, say, could marry a man, and so her freedom to marry is not denied, but only limited, is as equally persuasive as it defrauds the institution of marriage, promoting a "marriage" in form only, not in substance.[18]

The sexual orientation limitation, in addition to other restrictions traditionally taken to constitute the marriage relationship, affect and limit heterosexual couples as well. One family law scholar has argued against such limitations in his pursuit of "a new model of status. . . . how we might use status in a way that is sensitive to both the egalitarian ideal and the pluralistic character of contemporary family life."[19] Harry Krause sounds a similiar note regarding law's relation to the changing society it governs and must reflect:

> The Supreme Court emphasizes that marriage is a "fundamental human right," but new personal lifestyles and increasing opportunity for women to have full careers are reducing the importance of that right—even as same-sex partners, still excluded, may soon succeed in their quest for legal marriage. . . . Looking forward, we must adapt the legal concept of marriage and family not only to the decline of the "welfare state," but also to the diversity of lifestyles that are now lived and widely accepted. The traditional, unitary legal ramifications of marriage have not kept pace.[20]

Challenging the reasonableness of the heteroexclusivity of legal marriage, Milton Regan finds the sexual orientation limitation unethical, and urges that we make the marriage institution available to same-sex couples because the "moral aspiration that marriage has expressed is not heterosexual intimacy per se, but the more general vision of responsibility based on the cultivation of a relational sense of identity."[21] Regan admits that legal recognition of same-sex marriage "would not necessarily challenge stereotypes that denigrate homosexuals," but he does not find that or any other argument compelling enough to refrain from doing so.[22] The institution of marriage is constantly evolving, and there seems to be no *a priori* reason, apart from one grounded in a heterosexist sectarian perspective as regards the nature of marriage or homosexuality, for it not to be capable of accommodating "those with different differences."[23]

At any rate, marriage in the law is connected to a particular moral understanding of heterosexuality that makes it seem rightful to deny this civil status to gay persons.[24] Sociologist Jo VanEvery makes this point clear:

> The hegemonic form of heterosexuality is marriage. . . . Heterosexual acts usually take place within relationships. While they could take place in many different types of relationships, a particular type of heterosexual relationship is hegemonic in Western societies: lifelong, monogamous, cohabiting relationships, legally sanctioned through marriage and producing children. The hegemony of this type of heterosexual relationship is being challenged.[25]

Heterosexuality is a normative concept, not merely sexual, and that in a sectarian way, as we present it here.[26] A clarification of the ordinary understanding may be appropriate here.

"Sexual orientation" commonly refers to gay persons, who are homosexual. Usually the term "sexual orientation" is used to refer to gay persons, because they are different from the people who previously were not generally thought of as having a sexual orientation. Gay persons have a sexual orientation because they are different from heterosexuals, people who do not have a sexual orientation. Heterosexuality just is, it is assumed, whereas homosexuality is something special. It usually goes unremarked that heterosexuality, far from merely being a natural default category, is just as much a way of arranging things, concepts, and people as is homosexuality. Heterosexuality as such, as a multidimensional issue that indicates a class of persons, is almost always removed from the discussion; it is an underanalyzed, woefully underinvestigated area of scholarly inquiry.[27]

Heterosexism, a heterosexual-encoded preference in ethics and moral understanding, may lack what perhaps is most presumed of it, a biblical basis. The theologican and ethicist James Nelson describes heterosexism as a "deadly sin." "Tragically, this sin has pervaded both Jewish and Christian histories," and has tended to prevent the faithful from affirming the presence of the divine in alternative sexual practices that may well be as life-giving in the eyes of God.[28] It would be gross understatement to remark that the text and meaning of the Bible itself have been the subject of fierce debate and opposing interpretations, especially on the modern subject of sexual orientation.[29] Nonetheless, supporters of the traditional, heteronormative understanding of the institution of marriage pose unanimous on the religious dimension, perhaps because in this debate it is the only dimension the truth of which inherently resists empirical or public proof or disproof.[30]

Following the decision in *Baehr*, the Hawaii case, several states have advanced measures to inscribe heterosexual preference into their marriage laws, to make explicit what was in all but a handful of states unstated; these moves betray a heteronormative motive, or so we argue.[31] The next chapter reviews some recent events in the states, as well as the Defense of Marriage Act, that are based in a heterosexist sectarian preference for traditional marriage.

TWO

The Defense of Marriage Act and Recent Events in State Law

Frantic orthodoxy is never rooted in faith but in doubt. It is when we are not sure that we are doubly sure.[1]

Marriage in the law denotes a status founded on a civil contract. Today, marriage is also surrounded today by a heavy dose of politics, which is itself infused with traditional American religious beliefs regarding the institution of marriage, sexual norms, and sexuality.[2] The traditional understanding of marriage in the United States has maintained a significant religious sense, which some believers maintain is its kernel, its most treasured aspect, as in the following sample description:

> [T]he couple commit themselves to one another, but they also commit themselves *as a couple* to participate sacramentally and ministerially in the life of the Christian community; they commit to a shared discipleship. . . . This is the intrinsic reality of Christian marriage. . . . it reaches its significance to the divine. . . . A marriage exists eschatologically; it is tending toward its fulfillment beyond this world.[3]

Given the very definite religious pedigree of the preferred and legally enforced marital regime in the United States, American public law remains a site for the articulation of Christian religious values, burdening non-believers who may be resented, ironically, for having turned marriage into a political issue.[4]

On the matter of gay rights generally, however, American society is moving in another direction. One can read the six features of contemporary public law, the public policy considerations discussed in the Introduction, as on the whole an acknowledgment that gay Americans should have equal rights. In this chapter we present and discuss some recent events in state law and the 1996 Defense of Marriage Act or DOMA, which work against that progression towards greater inclusion and equal status through foreclosing the option of legal recognition of same-sex marriage. These actions in the law, their supporters implausibly suggest, do not reflect any animus towards any class of citizens; yet they turn on the notion that any dilution in legal preference for exclusively opposite-sex marriage betokens a bias against them.

Since the specter of same-sex marriage arose during the mid-1990s in the State of Hawaii, many states have sought to amend their marriage laws where they were unclear as to the gender eligibility requirements. These alterations of the law clarify a state's intent that the institution of marriage within that state is reserved for heterosexual couples, and cannot be extended to same-sex couples.[5] One effect of DOMA was to clarify the national legislature's intent that no state should have to recognize a same-sex marriage from another state.[6] In this chapter we review some of the articulated rationales behind these clarifications, which we will demonstrate are wanting for lack of a legitimate public purpose. The notion that a change in the law to allow for legal recognition of same-sex marriages, or reading the law so as to allow for such, would present a bureaucratic and financial burden, is an argument we do not take up. If the case for the legitimacy of same-sex marriages becomes convincing, and Americans decry the violation of a fundamental right or taken-for-granted liberty interest that will have been brought to light, then able policymakers will craft the appropriate legislation to facilitate the administrative and financial changes (if any) needed to enforce the new law.

In 1991, three same-sex couples filed a complaint against the State of Hawaii to protest being denied permission to obtain a marriage license. This case eventually went to the highest state court, which found in their favor.[7] The State of Hawaii attempted to defend its marriage law against the Court's decision, but was unsuccessful at doing so. On December 3, 1996, First Circuit Court of Hawaii Judge Kevin Chang declared the revised state ban on same-sex marriage to be unconstitutional in a 46-page decision. Judge Chang found that the state failed to show a compelling reason to justify the sex discrimination in its marriage law, and ordered it to issue marriage licenses to same-sex couples. On the following day, Judge Chang granted a state motion to delay implementation of his ruling pending another appeal by the state to the Hawaii state supreme court. Although the controversy was still in play in the state courts, the citizens of Hawaii in the meantime approved a ballot initiative that bans same-sex marriage, which will itself be challenged in court.[8]

In *Baehr*, the Supreme Court of Hawaii found that same-sex couples were discriminated against on the basis of their gender, a protected category meriting heightened scrutiny in the State of Hawaii, and not sexual orientation, an irrelevant consideration in this case. The court found the argument that marriage, by definition, precludes same-sex couples, as was urged on the Court in *Loving*, where the union at issue was construed as impossible because of a deity, "tautological and circular":

> With all due respect to the Virginia courts of a bygone era, we do not believe that trial judges are the ultimate authorities on the subject of Divine Will, and, as *Loving* amply demonstrates, constitutional law may mandate, like it or not, that customs change with an evolving social order.[9]

The *Baehr* court found that despite tradition's negative sanction of same-sex marriage, a same-sex couple ought not be discriminated against in applying for the same status and slate of benefits that the State of Hawaii grants to opposite-sex couples.

This court also found that, as in *Loving*, an unjust system (racism or sexism) was masquerading under the cover of a law that ostensibly treated everyone equally, because, were it not for the racial or gender classification at issue, the law would not then make sense. The *Baehr* court, however, did not find a fundamental right to same-sex marriage, or that homosexual persons constituted a suspect class, for the following reasons. First, regardless of sexual orientation, itself not the issue for this court, no-one has a fundamental right to same-sex marriage, in that this is not found in the Constitution, or specifically provided for in Hawaii state law. Secondly, the finding of discrimination based in a gender difference already triggered heightened scrutiny, as "sex" is a protected class in the State of Hawaii. It was not necessary to explore further whether sexual orientation ought to be considered a protected class, a judgment resting with the state legislature in any case.

At roughly the same time as in Hawaii, the marriage laws of the State of Alaska were being challenged on the basis of discriminating against same-sex couples. In the case of *Brause v. Bureau of Vital Statistics*, an Alaska Superior Court Judge ruled that the Alaska Constitution grants and protects the fundamental privacy right of each individual to choose his or her life partner.[10] This decision jolted the Alaska state legislature to propose and pass the Marriage Amendment to the

Alaska Constitution, revising the gender-neutral marriage statute expressly to prohibit same-sex marriages, as follows: "To be valid or recognized in this State, a marriage may exist only between one man and one woman."[11]

In both Hawaii and Alaska, there were live challenges to the law on behalf of the equal rights of same-sex couples to marry, and these challenges were, over the course of time in Hawaii, and rather quickly in Alaska, met with legislative actions that presumably safeguarded each state from this possibility. The events in another state, Vermont, took a different turn.

The State of Vermont, more recently, has also been embroiled in a controversy over its marriage laws with respect to same-sex couples. Vermont's State Constitution grants a greater measure of equal protection in the area of legally conferred state benefits than is true in most other states. In Vermont, *not* to grant state benefits to same-sex couples was seen as a violation that demanded redress. In *Stan Baker, et al. v. State of Vermont, et al.*, the Supreme Court of Vermont made the following important distinction between widely held beliefs, and constitutional commitments:

> May the State of Vermont exclude same-sex couples from the benefits and protections that its laws provide to opposite-sex married couples? That is the fundamental question we address in this appeal, a question that the Court well knows arouses deeply-felt religious, moral, and political beliefs.... The issue before the Court, moreover, *does not turn on the religious or moral debate over intimate same-sex relationships, but rather on the statutory and constitutional basis for the exclusion of same-sex couples from the secular benefits and protections offered married couples.*[12]

Basing its ruling in the "Common Benefits Clause" of Vermont's State Constitution, the Court found the exclusion of certain people from state-conferred benefits to violate "the inclusionary principle at its textual core," which mandates that benefits ought to be provided so as to provide "no Vermonter particular advantage."[13]

The State of Vermont, in defending its marriage statute against the same-sex challenge, proffered a variety of public policy considerations, several of which were contradicted in the context of Vermont's explicit gay rights provisions such as in employment, housing, and adoption.[14] The chief argument of the state was that to allow same-sex marriages would weaken the commitment between opposite-sex spouses who have children, and break the link between procreation and child rearing. The Court deemed the connection between allowing same-sex marriages and decoupling procreation from child rearing illogical, and found this line of reasoning unpersuasive and lacking in empirical warrant.[15] To the contrary, that a same-sex couple wishes to move their relationship into marriage, and possibly also to rear children, would seem to demonstrate their commitment, given the burdens and responsibilities for each other they are assuming. The alleged link has been decoupled in numerous opposite-sex marriages for reason of lack of ability or desire with respect to either procreation or child rearing, or both. The Court did not create a right to marry, but paved the way for the Vermont State Legislature to do so, which it then all but did under the rubric of "civil union," following the defeat of an effort to amend the state's constitution with a defense of marriage proposal as was passed in Alaska.[16]

Events in the states, and especially the legal actions in Hawaii, Alaska, and Vermont, discussed above, suggested to members of Congress that the nation might be well served were it to legislate on the matter at the national level. Although in the United States the regulation of the marriage relationship has always been reserved to the states, the encroaching possibility that ordinary comity among the states, reflected in the extension of full faith and credit by each state to each other's public laws, would soon come to expand the scope of legal recognition of same-sex marriage from Hawaii across the nation, triggered a nearly unprecedented congressional reaction.[17] This action was the Defense of Marriage Act or DOMA. It reads, in pertinent parts:

> No State, territory, or possession of the United States, or Indian tribe, shall be required to give effect to any public act, record, or judicial proceeding of may State, territory, possession, or tribe respecting a relationship between persons of the same sex that is treated as a marriage under the laws of such other State, territory, possession, or tribe, or a right or claim arising from such relationship.
>
> In determining the meaning of any Act of Congress, or of any ruling, regulation, or interpretation of the various administrative bureaus and agencies of the United States, the word "marriage" means only a legal union between one man and one woman as husband and wife, and the word "spouse" refers only to a person of the opposite sex who is a husband or a wife.[18]

The national legislature, then, not only defined the marriage relationship for federal purposes, but also regulated it definitionally for interstate purposes so as to prevent one state from being required to give full faith and credit to a legally recognized same-sex marriage from another state.

At the time DOMA was passed, no state extended legal recognition to same-sex marriage, nor has any state since. Federalism would suggest that each state be allowed to fashion its own marriage regulations, consistent with the federal guarantees of equal protection and due process as provided for in the Fourteenth Amendment.[19] Any state's duly enacted specific measure to ban same-sex marriage would likely qualify as a worthy, local public policy exception to the established customary rule of respecting the duly enacted acts of other states. A state with the ban in place would not simply be forced to accept marriages contrary to their own laws, at least not before its own laws had already fallen before a constitutional challenge that may not involve another state. Besides, even with DOMA now in place, a state can still choose to recognize same-sex marriages performed in another state. DOMA simply was *not* needed to shield the states from unwanted revolutions in their marriage and family law, or to allow states to liberalize their laws. Legal scholar Cass Sunstein put this point quite strongly in his oral testimony before the Senate Judiciary Committee on July 11, 1996:

> The full faith and credit clause, above all, has a unifying purpose, not a disunifying purpose.... This is an invalid form of legislation.... In conclusion, this legislation has never been—nothing like it has ever been done. It's unprecedented. It may well be pointless. This problem has been handled by the states for well over two hundred years. If it has a point, it risks unconstitutionality. From the standpoint of federalism and constitutional law, it is ill advised.[20]

The suggestion that something else was at work, motivating the proposal and passage of DOMA, is irresistible. It is at the federal level, itself rarely the site of any marriage regulation, that DOMA stands strongest as an expression in the law of heteroexclusivity.

Practically or strategically speaking, DOMA gives effect to a sneaking suspicion that a national standard as provided by the federal definition of marriage in DOMA would be the best armament to field in the face of a constitutional challenge to a state's ban on same-sex marriage. That is to say, when the expected challenge to a state's ban on same-sex marriage comes from a same-sex couple whose marriage has received legal recognition in another state, a challenge based in the fundamental right to marry as discussed in the previous chapter, a DOMA-like statute would provide the defense of the state's ban, which thereafter would provide the warrant for not abiding by the full faith and credit clause. DOMA recognized that each adult citizen's fundamental liberty interest in marriage must receive considerable weight, and that those states that pass bans on same-sex marriage might appear to have done so arbitrarily or, worse, specifically to fence out certain citizens from state-conferred benefits, as has been the case in the past, for example, with interracial marriages.[21]

As will be presented in Chapter Six, the legal definition of marriage need not be the one given in DOMA, nor need it reflect traditional practice and custom in this country, or in Western civilization generally. Congress could have written a more inclusive definition of marriage into law, one that had as its aim the extension of status and benefits to those persons, or couples, who, formerly, were denied them, and who regard themselves as married, and are considered married in the eyes of their community and by bonafide agents empowered by the State to marry. At any rate, that Congress could and did enact DOMA implies that the institution of marriage is subject to Congressional definition, as opposed to being fixed in stone as is the movement of the planets, or the course of water across the Earth.

At a more theoretical level, the element at work motivating the proposal and passage of DOMA is a heteronormative regime defending itself from a new idea in the marketplace. Below we quote from, and comment on, the core arguments made by several prominent Congressional supporters of DOMA, such as Congressman Robert Barr (R-GA):

> Enough is enough. Congress is drawing the line and saying marriage, as its been known for thousands of years, will remain the legal union between one man and one woman: nothing more and nothing less. . . . My bill says states will not be forced to accept same-sex marriage, and the federal government will take the straightforward step of defining marriage so no one may abuse a 2,000 year old understanding of what marriage is, and open the U.S. Treasury to raid by homosexual extremists determined to grant the whole range of federal benefits, including social security, or veterans' survivor benefits.[22]

Barr erroneously believes that marriage has remained fundamentally unchanged for 2,000 years, and that defending marriage as per this understanding is in itself a legitimate governmental purpose, and a fiscally sound one at that.[23] Since the United States Constitution does not draw, or imply a line between "Americans" and "homosexuals," Barr's is not a straightforward step unless the moral understanding it reflects is constitutionally privileged, which it is not, and at the least cannot be where fundamental rights and liberty interests are trampled on.

Senator Dan Coats' (R-IN) statements barely veil the *shadow establishment:*

> The definition of marriage is not created by politicians and judges, and it cannot be changed by them. It is rooted in our history, our laws, our deepest moral and religious convictions, and our nature as human beings. . . . Our urgent responsibility is to nurture and strengthen that institution, not undermine it with trendy moral relativism. . . . The preservation of marriage has become an issue of self-preservation for our society.[24]

Senator Coats does not appreciate the irony of the context for the statements he makes, politicians selecting to legislate a definition of marriage, politically motivated to render into law the correct point-of-view. Whether American citizens who happen to be gay or lesbian, those Americans who support them, and those clergy who marry them, are "moral relativists" who fail to recognize "our nature as human beings," is beyond the ken of the Senate to discern, and cannot provide a basis for lawmaking.

A longtime foe of equal rights for Americans who are gay or lesbian, Senator Jesse Helms (R-GA), submitted the following remarks:

> Indeed, Mr. President, the pending bill . . . will safeguard the sacred institutions of marriage and the family from those who would seek to destroy them and who are willing to tear apart America's moral fabric in the process. Isn't it disheartening, Mr. President, that Congress must clarify the traditional definition of marriage?[25]

Senator Helms' comments reflect an insecurity about the solidness of traditional marriage, and a failure of moral imagination to see gay relationships as inherently good, as other kinds are assumed to be. His view is that there can only be one marital regime in the United States, because the presence of any other will wreck its quality of being sacred, or destroy the American family outright. An alternative approach to comprehending formalized same-sex relationships would be to see gay persons as embracing the traditional goods of the marital relationship they desperately wish to enter.

The Senate's synopsis of pro-DOMA arguments was twofold.[26] First, those favoring passage noted the decay of civilization and the need for two-parent families to maintain it. The traditional values associated with the family are given as "prudence, temperance, fortitude, justice, faith, hope, and love," which are institutionalized in the sacred institution of marriage, other lifestyles being sinful. DOMA would act to prevent the further decline of American civilization and family life, and mitigate against lawsuits among the states where uniformity does not obtain regarding same-sex marriage. Second, DOMA supporters in the Senate believed that it strengthens the possibility that state legislatures, and not state courts with their unelected judges, will decide for each state the policy on same-sex marriage.

The first pro-DOMA argument falters because, as presented in the Introduction, increasingly more states have a variety of pro-gay policies connected to family life that put the lie to the claim that same-sex relationships, or "homosexuality," and "family" are inimical. The values said to surround opposite-sex marriage and family life are human values, hardly exclusive to one or the other sexual orientation. In addition, uniformity was not obtained previously in marriage laws across the states, given differences in honoring common law marriages, stipulations regarding degrees of relationship, racial categories, and other differences.

The second pro-DOMA argument, if sincere, could just as easily have been accomplished by a legislative act that allowed for each state to decide the question for itself, the federal government's definition notwithstanding, rather than specifying same-sex marriage as that one policy preference which states cannot be compelled to recognize. Congress could have specified marriage more generally, as between two adults of any gender or sexual orientation, rather than cater to traditional majoritarian values that rest uncomfortably in the law in a liberal-democratic regime.[27]

The Defense of Marriage Act, in the eyes of its congressional supporters, appears more to "defend" a traditional understanding of the Christian moral point-of-view, than to achieve a legitimate public purpose. DOMA more reflects a distaste for the lifestyles of certain Americans and those state laws that specifically protect them in their rights and liberties, than it actually supports an ostensibly beleaguered institution. The recent events in state law and DOMA suggest a reassertion of traditional American morality in the law, through prohibitions against same-sex marriage that are unequivocal. The exception of the advances in Vermont suggests that the absolutist stance of this morality and the laws reflecting it are not universally recognized or desired, and that American society need not be wedded to them.[28]

Later chapters will argue that this reassertion and its manifestation in the law are, in reality, *not* in keeping with the American political regime, and should be rejected for complete want of legitimate public purpose. Interestingly, the Justice who first inserted the phrase that the United States is "a Christian nation" into the legal lexicon meant by that to state a fairly comprehensive social fact, *not* to set a legal precedent for future constructions of the spirit of the laws. For Justice

Brewer, legislating on the basis of the United States being "a Christian nation" would *not* be in keeping with the American political regime, or so argues one church-state law expert.[29]

The real issue behind the ban on same-sex marriage in both Hawaii and Alaska, as well as in the Defense of Marriage Act, is the values that are said to be advanced, that give the ban its sense of rightfulness, of being "good." All of these actions in the law lack the cachet of values each American citizen can rightfully expect under the rule of law, such as the equality and due process guarantees of the Fourteenth Amendment. These actions reflect many people's concern that their heteronormative understanding of the institution of marriage be esconced in the law, with the immediate and intended effect of fencing out certain of their fellow citizens from legally entering into that relationship. Can the blunt instrument of the legal ban on same-sex marriage simply uphold a conscientiously held, heteronormative conviction, to the detriment of the rights and liberty interests of others, because its supporters believe it is under threat?

Some of the ban's supporters make the claim that the ban is necessary to maintain not just the "sanctity" of the traditional understanding of marriage, but its exclusivity as well. One supporter of the traditional view advances the following line of argument:

> Validating same-sex marriages would sow confusion.... Traditional marriage is encouraged by treating it as unique, which it would not be if same-sex marriages were treated equally. Therefore, the main consequence of recognizing same-sex marriage would not be a shift of some people to homosexual conduct, but the change in heterosexuals' no longer seeing traditional marriage as something special.... The religious associations of marriage are important even to unbelievers; many who otherwise never enter a church or temple still insist on being married there.... If these honors [the honors conferred by law] were granted liberally, they would be cheapened.... Validating gay marriage would break the link of marriage to the divine, to the miracle of creation of new life, and to the rich tradition of love and commitment between husbands and wives.[30]

The just-quoted line of reasoning would connect to the ban on same-sex marriage, only if the law were the property of just those persons who subscribe to the traditional view. This mustn't be the case, because, though a democracy, law in the United States has carved out a wide range of rights and liberty interests the protection of which is especially important in the case of dissenters to received custom, with the heteronormative understanding of marriage being one such custom.

The traditional view of marriage currently finds itself in a marketplace of ideas, and faced with public discussion about the suitability of a new form of the marital relationship. Its supporters wish to see that market closed, to the extent that it is a free market. At other points in our history the traditional perspective has found itself competing with other marital regimes of one sort or another, using the law to close off the market in ways that now are regarded as odious, such as bans on interracial marriage.[31] The perception that supporters of traditional opposite-sex marriage may have, that same-sex marriage will come to erode or rival their own, or crowd out their preferred moral point-of-view, undercutting the goodness of the the marital relationship, are starved for lack of empirical warrant. They ought to fail to persuade the American citizenry as a whole to embody in the law a denigration of gay persons and their relationships by proscribing their quest legally to validate their relationships.

The freedom of religious expression of supporters of the traditional view would be under threat only if they were coerced somehow into joining in same-sex marriages against their religious dictates. Absent the legitimate use of the coercive power of the State to prevent a person from entering into a marriage that goes against his or her religious beliefs, as is not ordinarily the case today, or likely ever to be the case, the State can only illegitimately legislate to protect the preferred moral point of view held by traditionalists. This is exactly what the State has done, both in several states and through DOMA, serving a political and religious majority, but perhaps not in the best interests of all Americans.

Viewed politically, the events in the states, as discussed above, and DOMA, reflect a sharp cleavage in American society between politically active religious traditionalists and a fairly apolitical irreligious minority.[32] The Republican Party, argues political scientist Gregory Layman in a comprehensive empirical study, has succumbed to the "Christian Right," with which it has bonded and which, in turn, uses the GOP as its last, best hope of retarding the trend towards an increasingly secular society in the United States.[33] Layman views the gradual conjuncture of religious with political conservatism at the level of one of the nation's two major political parties with dread:

> It is clear that the cultural battles that have raged in American party politics over the last three decades constitute far and away the most important reason for the current connection between traditionalist-modernist religious orientations on the one hand and ideological-modernist leanings, partnership, and voting decisions on the other hand. . . . The manifestation of the contemporary religious conflict in party politics may have implications beyond the

religious composition of the parties' coalitions and the parties' stands on cultural issues. . . . It even may have consequences for the health of American democracy.[34]

Political theorist Rogers Smith also sounds a gloomful note in his assessment of the potential of those Americans who are irreligious to have their voice heard:

> [T]he outlooks that are most at risk of being denied genuine public respect in the United States today, as throughout our history, especially include beliefs that are overtly critical of much conventional religiosity. . . . Instead, any hint that views opposed to prevailing religions might gain overt political primacy triggers powerful opposition. . . . Now as ever, it is secular outlooks explicitly opposed to basic religious beliefs that come closest to being silenced in contemporary public discussions. Hence, these, along with genuinely unconventional religious viewpoints, are the ones that courts must be most concerned to safeguard.[35]

Smith likens the fears and disadvantages of the irreligious in the American context to "second-class citizenship," an illegitimate status that may best describe the one occupied by American citizens who happen to be gay or lesbian.[36]

Our argument is that the recent actions in the law, as well as DOMA, do *not* exemplify the kind of laws we Americans ought to enact, or ought to have govern us, because they reflect a point of view that does not merit the state's grant of exclusivity. Not to appreciate the nature of the rationale supporting the ban is not to understand it, because no public policy considerations can provide the muscle necessary to overcome the liberty interest at stake—that of an adult to marry the loved one of her choice, not the religious and political majority's liberty interest in maintaining the exclusivity of a sectarian heteronormative understanding of the marital relationship.

Given the assumption that our earlier presentation of the six features of the law in a good many jurisdictions below the federal level exhausted any possibly legitimate secular purpose of a heteroexclusive marriage law, into what category does the heteronormative motive fall, such as animates the Defense of Marriage Act? Part II takes up the issues of the relationship between law and morality (Chapter Three), and the impermissible entrenching in the law of a sectarian preference in violation of liberty of conscience (Chapter Four).

PART II

The Law and Morality Distinction, Violated

In the following chapters we will find that supporters of the ban against same-sex marriage resist not only the inevitable evolution of the marital relationship, but also the liberal-democratic ideals of this nation. They represent a sectarian-inspired majoritarian threat to American democratic values as vouchsafed in the nation's constitutionally ordered republic, one that features religious pluralism and protection of dissent from any or all religious obligations, as well as legal sensitivity to the imposition of religious scruples. This latter idea was outlined by Justice Felix Frankfurter in 1943:

> When dealing with religious scruples we are dealing with an almost numberless variety of doctrines and beliefs entertained with equal sincerity.... The great leaders of the American Revolution were determined to remove political support from every religious establishment.... So far as the state was concerned, there was to be neither orthodoxy nor heterodoxy.... The constitutional protection of religious freedom terminated disabilities, it did not create new privileges.... Any person may therefore believe or disbelieve what he pleases.... Religion is outside the sphere of political government.... It would be too easy to cite numerous prohibitions and injunctions to which laws run counter if the variant interpretations of the Bible were made the tests of obedience to law. The validity of secular laws cannot be measured by their conformity to religious doctrines. It is only in a theocratic state that ecclesiastical doctrines measure legal right or wrong.[1]

The reasoning in Justice Frankfurter's dissenting opinion in Board of Education v. Barnette *highlights two aspects of religion and morals discourse about which the civil authority as such is obliged to decline making any substantive determinations. First, one must ask the question, with which or whose religious scruples are we dealing? And, second, how can we incorporate into law any particular, discrete* religious prescription simply on its own merits, without incorporating any or all of the rest and so run the risk of becoming more ecclesiastical than civil? Or, are we better to ask, is the one East, the other West, and to grant differences in degree already places us on one or the other side of the distinction in kind between the twain, even where we believe ourselves to see only an expanding middle? Frankfurter's explication suggests that the motivation to balance interests in this area is ill-advised, and urges maximally cautious skepticism at even the most seemingly innocous of accommodations. On this line of reasoning, each tiny step to accommodate religious expression, no matter how stringent, is fraught with an extreme risk of establishment.

The two chapters that follow turn on the plausible proposition that the determination "homosexuality is wrong" presumes a certain morals regime that is neither reducible to the criminal law, nor an edifying part of law in a constitutionally ordered republic. Our emphasis here is twofold, both on the important particular points put forth, and on the links between them. Realizing this emphasis requires presenting a few lengthy, representative chains of reasoning. Space does not permit a lengthy elaboration of the modern debate concerning morals and the law; the literature here is voluminous and received arguably its most important formulation in John Stuart Mill's essay **On Liberty**. Mill was concerned with the fallibility of human beings, who not only frequently succumb to the lure of absolute truth, but, and politically more on point, also give in to the temptation to legislate on that basis alone. Religion is a likely candidate for absolutely certain absolute truth. The necessity for a population to have the "right" religion has been one of history's greatest troublemaking motivations, especially when pursued with enthusiasm.[2]

The morals regime that gives sense to the new national ban on same-sex marriage is a religiously inspired heteronormative order that has subjected its non-heterosexual of citizens to administration by the civil authority, where other citizens are not burdened. While distinguishing moral from political sense in controversy over permissible grounds for denial of the right to marry, an aspect of a larger concern, the philosopher Martha Nussbaum opines: "I believe that the rights of lesbians and gays are a central issue of justice for our time."[3] The larger concern is the equal status of all citizens, the central principle of the U.S. Constitution, or so Karst has argued:

> The principle of equal citizenship . . . means this: Each individual is presumptively entitled to be treated by the organized society as a respected,

responsible, and participating member. Stated negatively, the principle forbids the organized society to treat an individual as a member of an inferior or dependent caste or as a nonparticipant.[4]

Heteronormativity insistently would make humanity and heterosexuality synonymous, and render homosexuality or any alternative construction of sexuality morally objectionable.[5]

Heteronormativity seems to be losing its tight grip in even mainline Christian churches in the United States, where a contentious dialogue is taking place that includes a fair amount of opposition to the universalism of the heterosexual ideal, as well as noteworthy initiatives to fully include gays and lesbians as such as part of the Christian commitment to God, love, and justice.[6] *Exposing the heteronormative regime behind its manifestations in everyday practice through "homophobia" and "heterosexism" requires unveiling the religiously-rooted morals edifice that provides its animating rationale and makes "intuitive" sense even when it is not named.*[7] *And where heterosexuality as a value is seen to undergird the law and to conflict with other values, then it becomes a matter of weighing the values to see where the preponderance of public commitment ought to rest. The next two chapters lay out the claim that the preponderance properly rests elsewhere, on the American commitments to equality, the rule of law, and, not least, freedom of religion considered importantly to include disestablishment.*

THREE

Morals Discourse and Law

The medieval historian Mark D. Jordan has forcefully argued that the term "sodomy" was invented by the eleventh century theologian Peter Damian for a specific purpose, one unconnected with same-sex sexual activities, and that its widely assumed resonance with a time-immemorial tradition is unsupported by the facts. Rather, history reveals the theological incoherence of the blithely presumed stable category of "sodomy."[1] Nonetheless, in modern times "sodomite," describing a person who performs an illicit sexual act, has been used interchangeably with "homosexual," and now also with "gay," so as to lend support to the idea that the gay person might be for all purposes a criminal, even beyond sexual conduct.[2]

We begin this discussion with a quotation from William Blackstone's *Commentaries on the Laws of England* the *locus classicus* in Anglo-American law regarding sodomitical behavior, the activity that has tended to be taken best to characterize homosexual persons:

> IV. What has been here observed, especially with regard to the manner of proof, which ought to be more clear in proportion as the crime is the more detestable, may be applied to another offense, of a still deeper malignity [than rape]; the infamous *crime against nature*, committed either with man or beast. A crime which ought to be strictly and impartially proved, and then as strictly and impartially punished. But it is an offense of so dark a nature. . . . I will not act so disagreeable a part, to my readers as well as myself, as to dwell any longer upon a subject, the very mention of which is a disgrace to human nature. It will be more eligible to imitate in this respect the delicacy of our English law, which treats it, in its very indictments, as a crime not fit to be named [among Christians]. . . . This is the voice of nature and of reason, and the express law of God, determined to be capital. Of which we have a signal instance long before the Jewish dispensation, by the destruction of two cities by fire from heaven; so that this is an universal, not merely a provincial precept.[3]

Blackstone goes on to describe the punishments familiar to him, which include "commanding such miscreant to be burnt to death. . . . buried alive" and hanging, for this offense of greater magnitude than rape, another felony, by contrast with the "inferior offences or misdemeanors, that fall under this head . . . *assaults, batteries, wounding, false imprisonment,* and *kidnapping.*"[4]

The passages from Blackstone have all the hallmarks of morals legislation: the offense is ambiguously described, yet it arouses the passions; there is no statement of actual harm to anyone, but of presumed harm to generalized sensibilities which the law aims to protect, here even in its utterance; its relation to other criminal acts where there is harm seems exaggerated out of proportion, as is the level of punishment inflicted; it attempts to describe things as they objectively exist, but indicates how they are is given to us by God, the law's ultimate source; a measure of justification is secured by the pretense of universalism, here clearly of a particular tradition; an attempt is made to veil its embedded morality. In addition, any success at prevention of the offense or educating a population away from it on this textual basis is open to serious question, assuming *arguendo* these purposes. The Chief Justice's concurring opinion in the *Bowers* case quoted from Blackstone and remarked that "[c]ondemnation of these practices is firmly rooted in Judeo-Christian moral and ethical standards."[5] In *Bowers* a sectarian tradition supplied the moral reasoning behind the technical law findings in that case, and shows Blackstone's influence. In his written opinions Burger has frequently deferred to the majoritarianism of an existing community, rather than to the individual pressing a rights claim against it, as one might expect in the American context.[6]

In a word, discrimination based on sexual orientation *is* morals legislation, religious in nature and arbitrary from another point of view, over which it exercises hegemony. Now, should government have the power to legislate this morals perspective to the detriment of constitutionally guaranteed liberties such as the right to marry?

To some, homosexuality elicits a visceral response, and gay persons are detestable violators of the moral order, which they are taken to threaten. For such persons, this is insurmountable, "an issue of first impression," and the law legitimately can compel this moral feeling.[7] It was on this point, a point devolving on passion rather than reason, that Lord Justice Patrick Devlin and legal philosopher H. L. A. Hart had a famous, thoroughgoing debate during the 1960s.[8] The impetus to their discussion was a just-published report on homosexual behavior and the criminal law. The *Wolfenden Report*'s committee undertook its task in 1950s Britain; among the findings that disturbed readers inclined to legislate their morality are the following:

> Certain forms of sexual behavior are regarded by many as sinful, morally wrong, or objectionable for reasons of conscience, or of religious or cultural tradition. . . . But the criminal law does not cover all such actions at the present time. . . . We appreciate that opinions will differ as to what is offensive, injurious or inimical to the common good. . . . we should not wish to dogmatize, for on the matters with which we are called upon to deal we have not succeeded in discovering an unequivocal "public opinion," and we have felt bound to try to reach conclusions for ourselves rather than to base them on what is often transient and seldom precisely ascertainable.[9]

> To reverse a long-standing tradition is a serious matter and not to be suggested lightly. But the task entrusted to us . . . is to state what we regard as just and equitable law. . . . Unless a deliberate attempt is made by society, acting through the agency of the law, to equate the sphere of crime with that of sin, there must remain a realm of private morality and immorality which is, in brief and crude terms, not the law's business. . . . We accordingly recommend that homosexual behavior between consenting adults in private should no longer be a criminal offense.[10]

Moved to respond to the *Wolfenden Report*, Devlin wrote:

> Immorality, then, for the purpose of the law, is what every right-minded person is presumed to consider immoral. Any immorality is capable of affecting society injuriously and in effect to a greater or lesser extent it usually does. . . . I do not think one can ignore disgust if it is deeply felt and not manufactured. . . . There is, for example, a general abhorrence of homosexuality. . . . If that is the general feeling of the society in which we live, I do not see how society can be denied the right to eradicate it. . . . The limits of tolerance shift. . . . By the next generation the swell of indignation may have abated and the law be left without the strong backing which it needs. But it is then difficult to alter the law without giving the impression that moral judgment is being weakened. This is now one of the factors that is strongly militating against any alteration to the law on homosexuality.[11]

Hart was not taken with Devlin's rendering of the relationship between law and the enforcement of morality, especially not Devlin's likening of homosexual activity to political subversion such as treason.[12] This passage sums up the sense of Hart's reply:

> Indeed much that he writes reads like an abjuration of the notion that reasoning or thinking has much to do with morality. English popular morality has no doubt its historical connection with the Christian religion. . . . But it does

not owe its present status or social significance to religion any more than to reason. What is it then? According to Sir Patrick it is primarily a matter of feeling.[13]

Hart is also puzzled by the sort of feeling Devlin seems to wish people engaged when determining morals legislation, given that Devlin captures "ignorance, superstition, or misunderstanding," rather than appeals to "reason, sympathetic understanding, as well as critical intelligence."[14] Contemporary legal philosopher Ronald Dworkin has also taken issue with Devlin's broader thesis, questioning the latter's reliance on the average man as a morally sound basis for making ethical judgments, or for determining the criminal law, and arguing that he does not understand what it is to disapprove on moral principle.[15]

The institution of marriage is, for Devlin, both Christian and non-Christian, depending on where one enters his circle of reasoning:

> In England we believe in the Christian idea of marriage and therefore adopt monogamy as a moral principle. Consequently, the Christian institution of marriage has become the basis of family life and so part of the structure of our society. It is there not because it is Christian. It has got there because it is Christian, but it remains there because it is built into the house into which we live and could not be removed without bringing it down. The great majority of those who live in this country accept it because it is the Christian idea of marriage and for them the only true one. But a non-Christian is bound by it, not because it is part of Christianity but because, rightly or wrongly, it has been adopted by the society in which he lives. It would be useless for him to stage a debate . . . if he wants to live in the house, he must accept it as built in the way in which it is.[16]

We can ask many questions of Devlin's presentation, such as who is this "we" who all live here "in the house"? Why does social convention or existing custom have the status of basic law? And, perhaps most importantly, why not discuss the "rightly or wrongly" dimension? But we need not engage all of this, for some things absent in Britain are clear in the American context.

In England there is no constitutional separation of church and state, (there is a state church), nor is there the American scheme of separation of powers and other filters such as judicial review that are designed to prevent majoritarian preferences from obtaining a presumptive sway in political debate. But Devlin nevertheless hints at what in the United States is the *shadow establishment* when he writes of marriage having "got there because it is Christian," and having remained there in a context of futility facing those who would open it up for debate.[17] One wonders whether in this country too the institution of marriage remains closed to gay persons because of strong negative sentiments regarding homosexuality that are determinative, and are taken to constitute a principled basis because they seem so very appropriate to the embedded religious preference that remains in the institution of marriage, once having got there.

The morals discourse that Blackstone once catalogued and that Devlin more recently exemplified fails to meet the requirements of liberal constitutionalism, which, in the first instance, is about the rule of law, by which is meant the U.S. Constitution and not some "higher law."[18] Yet, this morals discourse has persisted alongside liberal constitutionalism into the present day.[19] One legal scholar succinctly puts an alleged immorality in its place in the scheme of well-ordered liberty in a democratic society under the rule of law:

> [A]ny rational person, if thus compelled to dissect critically the reasons why he believes homosexuality to be immoral, will find that all he is left with are two; (1) homosexual intercourse is forbidden by the Bible; and (2) homosexuality engenders confusion of roles between the sexes and therefore arouses uneasiness, especially in those who require certainty of role definition. . . . But the former of these cannot claim to be anything more than a religious taboo . . . which hardly justifies legal sanctions by a secular state. . . . The point then is that whatever be the basis on which the collective judgment of society deprives one of its members of his freedom, it must be rationally defensible. Otherwise, a consensus has been violated that is even more fundamental to a democratic society than its shared ideas on any subject.[20]

To the extent that the morals of the common man are a composite of irrational factors, and that majoritarian morality may have inscribed features of intolerance, animosity, or prejudice, those morals fail to satisfy the rational basis test for determining a statute's constitutionality. Recently, Colorado's Amendment Two, a ballot initiative, was struck down by the Supreme Court for failing to meet this minimal test of legitimate governmental purpose:

> Amendment Two fails, indeed defies, even this conventional inquiry. . . . the amendment seems inexplicable by anything but animus towards the class that it affects; it lacks a rational relationship to legitimate state interests. . . . It is not within our constitutional tradition to enact laws of this sort. Central both to the idea of the rule of law and to our own Constitution's guarantee of equal protection is the principle that government and each of its parts remain open on impartial terms to all who seek its assistance. . . . We cannot say that Amendment 2 is directed to any identifiable legitimate purpose or discrete objective.[21]

Encoding the law with a non-rational understanding of morality is an arbitrary exercise of political power, no matter the extent of the majoritarian sentiment or fit with this or that way of life the statute can claim. One legal scholar, now federal judge, G. Sidney Buchanan, shifts the issue from unreasoned, odious majoritarianism to the majority's rightful concern for moral excellence, which legal and social recognition of same-sex marriage would threaten because opposite-sex marriage has been determined to be the bedrock standard of moral excellence, and so its exclusiveness must be maintained in the law.[22] Yet, oddly, the majority Buchanan relies on seems weak and in need of props:

> [T]he majority needs to know that the legal system, and especially the legislative process, may be used to promote the standards of morality to which the majority aspires. Without that assurance, the zeal to achieve moral excellence slackens, and the task of promoting moral excellence may fall into hands less friendly to the interests of society.[23]

Buchanan's argument against same-sex marriage is that it undermines pre-existing, foundational majority rule, and endangers society's heteroexclusive establishment through its appeal, which threatens the moral climate, as though morally straight heterosexual men would be attracted to a same-sex marriage. The dearth of evidence to support these contentions hardly needs mentioning, nor does the vagueness of determinations of "moral excellence," or the appropriateness of tailoring the criminal law simply to suit longstanding majority preference, at least in the American context.[24]

From Blackstone down through Devlin, a normative, heteroexclusive view of marriage has endured fairly intact despite the changes in legal regime witnessed during this period.[25] In the West one can trace the emergence of the Christian religion's dominance of marriage and family life initially by ecclesiastical control over their meaning and structure through the institutional practices of the Catholic Church. This dominance has stood as a countervailing force to the evolution and adaptations one anticipates in the history of any human institution, and has controlled more or less for any emerging challenges to its maintenance of an essence to the institution of marriage. Nonetheless, one scholarly study of this emergence has left some doubt as to whether the commonly understood rules governing the institution of marriage indicate an essence at all:

> The "morality" of the family that we have inherited has to be seen against the background of the accepted practices in earlier societies and the way in

which these were set aside or encouraged by the Church.... For the Church to grow and survive it had to accumulate property, which meant acquiring control over the way it was passed from one generation to the next. Since the distribution of property between generations is related to patterns of marriage and the legitimation of children, the Church had to gain authority over these so that it could influence the strategies of heirship. This essay has attempted to show how this came about and what it brought about.[26]

Were it not for the perception of divine sanction somewhere along the line, the same-sex marriage ban would not have endured in practice, or been legislated, as it serves no purpose other than to continue to register the majority's received sectarian preference, though today the formation of the law and the nature of the governing regime are different than they were centuries ago.

The argument can be made that this particular sort of preference, should it take the form of a faction, was specifically targeted by our constitutional founders. This is certainly the case in *The Federalist No. 10*, where James Madison defined faction and cautioned against the special danger of religion degenerating into a political faction, or, worse, zealotry, which tends not to admit of worldly limits. Here, religion is singled out for special mention because of its basis in the passions, not in reason, and special mention *not* for its being an unqualified good.[27] In the history of political philosophy Thomas Hobbes can be credited with the first major exposition of religious passion as an inherently worrisome, and destabilizing threat to the peace.[28] More recently, political scientist Ted Jelen has argued that publicly endorsed religion is a danger to social life and corrosive of political deliberation and public discourse in the setting of American democracy.[29]

The more or less unchanged, traditional religious view of marriage as legitimately restricted through law to heterosexual union has not kept up with the times, specifically, the following important changes engendered by citizenship in a liberal constitutional regime: religious pluralism and separation of church and state. Political theorist Gaus puts the new *Zeitgeist* this way:

> This liberal conviction—that impositions of religion were defeated—evolved into a more general conviction that justifications for imposing ways of living were also defeated. To be sure, this is an idea even more vague than that of establishment.... It does, though, seem to rule out claims that any relatively specific ways of living—in terms not only of God to be worshipped, but of occupations to be followed, personal ideals to be embraced, and so on—can be justifiably imposed on us.... Freedom of religion, and

more generally freedom of conscience, constitutes a recognition that certain issues are off the public agenda.[30]

These changes also affect the character of the regime's politics, which David Richards, a leading theorist of toleration, contrasts with our own:

> Such politics tends to degrade to forms of irrationalism in order to protect its now essentially polemical project: opposing views relevant to reasonable public argument are suppressed, facts distorted or misstated, values disconnected from ethical reasoning, and ultimately, deliberation in politics is denigrated in favor of violence against dissent.... Such politics enforced sectarian conceptions of religious, moral, and political truth at the expense of denying the moral powers of persons to assess these matters in light of reasonable standards and as reasonable persons.... The principle of toleration thus limits the force in *political* life of convictions that draw their strength solely from the certainties of group loyalty and identification ... .[31]

Viewed pessimistically, a constitutionally ordered, liberal-democratic regime such as the United States can ill-afford to chart a course through intolerant sectarian waters, given its fundamental philosophical commitments. Viewed more optimistically, the contemporary, highly diverse United States can do better by its diverse citizenry when it avoids such murky waters and seeks to affirm for all of them, rather than to deny some of them basic rights and liberties.

The nature of law in the liberal-democratic constitutional regime notwithstanding, contemporary commentators frequently evoke a morals discourse such as earlier propounded by Blackstone and Devlin. The following passages from a contemporary conservative observer are evocative in that way, though they no more artfully navigate the murky waters than did his predecessors:

> The Hebrew Bible, in particular the Torah ... has done more to civilize the world than any other book or idea in history.... Therefore, when this Bible makes strong moral proclamations, I listen with great respect. And regarding male homosexuality—female homosexuality is not mentioned—this Bible speaks in such clear and direct language that one does not have to be a religious fundamentalist in order to be influenced by its views.... Accepting homosexuality as the social, moral, or religious equivalent of heterosexuality would constitute the first modern assault on the extremely hard-won, millennia-old battle for a family-based, sexually monogamous society.... And the bedrock of this civilization, and of Jewish life, of course, has been the centrality and purity of family life. But the family is not a natural unit so much as a *value* that must be cultivated and protected ... At stake is our civilization.[32]

The constitutionality of legislation based on the "value" contained in the above excerpt, in the light of its "roots, purposes, and assumptions," can be held to serious doubt, "[f]or the morality that these laws would protect can trace a discernible path back to origins in religious authority."[33] Where secular interests do not obtain, this seems more of a case of respecting an establishment of religion than of advancing a legitimate public purpose, because the legal proscriptions at issue would not be sensible were it not for the rationale supplied by the given morals perspective. That is to say, there is no plausibly neutral, nonsectarian way to ascribe legitimacy to legislative prohibitions from that basis, neither to their causes nor to their effects.

Justice Antonin Scalia differs on this point: "Our society prohibits, and all human societies have prohibited, certain activities not because they harm others but because they are considered, in the traditional phrase, 'contra bonos mores,' i.e., immoral." And for that which is immoral *per se*, "absent specific constitutional protection for the conduct involved, the Constitution does not prohibit them [morals statutes] simply because they regulate 'morality.'"[34] Presumably, the Constitution could have been concerned to protect, say, cockfighting (one of Scalia's examples), and the most cockfighters can properly claim is profound disappointment that it was not concerned therewith. Scalia's analogy fails to persuade, however, because of the present constitutional status of the right to marriage, versus that of cockfighting, even should the underlying argument's circular form, resting on the assertion that an activity is immoral *per se*, be persuasive to those adherents of that perspective who are willing to deny the right at issue. The ban's direct and substantial interference with the exercise of a basic right or liberty interest requires independent public justification that allows for empirical validation of any claims made.

In this chapter we have distinguished morals discourse from another type, constitutionally permitted discourse, and criticized the former when it fails to meet the requirements each American citizen can rightfully expect of law, that it displays fairness to all citizens rooted in a constitutional conception of limited government, equality before the law, and the protection of equal laws, without an establishment of religion or arbitrary rule. The ban on same-sex marriage reflects an antecedent social morality that is sectarian in nature and falls most heavily on individual gay persons, violating their status in equal citizenship through denying their fundamental right or liberty interest in marriage. The ban and its effects are of a highly dubious ethical and legal nature, given the modern American context. That is to say, given the constitutionally specified ends of society.... [t]his means that citizens do not think there are antecedent social ends that justify them in viewing some people as having more or less worth to society than others and assigning them different basic rights and privileges accordingly. Many past societies have thought otherwise.[35]

Marriage, as we have seen, is taken by some to be so rooted in a particular morals regime as to preclude gay persons from its embrace for "reason" of the latter's being unnatural, perverse, sinful, and, perniciously ironical, unable to form long-term relationships, such as a marriage, the divorce rate of opposite-sex couples notwithstanding. Put differently, only a private, non-secular rationale makes sense of where the law has placed the outer limits of the marriage relationship. This may be an instance of faction-based, sectarian majoritarianism promoting a value, the sense of which is internal to religious convictions and should not be given legal effect in a constitutionally ordered, liberal-democratic republic such as the United States, especially if its legal effect, far from benign, burdens a fundamental liberty interest of some American citizens.

FOUR

Professor Richards Finds a Violation

My own mind is my own church.[1]

The shape we give to constitutional arguments constructs the shape of our moral identity as lesbian and gay persons, and we must responsibly define ourselves in the way most adequate to the common grievances of our diverse lives and experiences. The appeal to the right to conscience is . . . compelling because it most responsibly articulates our common grievances, and thus our demands for self-respect which will not acquiesce again in the silence of the grave assigned to us by the dominant religio-cultural orthodoxy that we challenge and must challenge.[2]

For a considerable period of Western history, during which Christianity was well established through the Catholic Church, statements such as in the first quotation, above, were regarded as heretical, somewhat as we earlier saw Blackstone and Devlin regarded gay persons, or at least homosexual activity. The freedom to hold heretical beliefs, for example, and to make such statements is not encompassed in any notion of religious tolerance that is respectful of the genuine sentiments expressed in Paine's statement. Rather, this freedom is what we with many of the constitutional framers understand as *liberty of conscience,* though they may well have seen this liberty manifested only in religious beliefs. Liberty of conscience evolved during the Enlightenment period alongside liberalism itself. John Locke's progressive sense of toleration, which nonetheless excluded atheists and Catholics, was an important step along the way.[3] Because this freedom encompasses irreligion as well as positively non-religious sentiment that might be countermajoritarian, it is a greater freedom than is freedom of religion;

so too is its principle of toleration. The lesser, religious principle of toleration has taken the following form, suggests political theorist Brian Barry: "Protestants and Catholics might agree to set their differences aside and allow freedom of worship, and then combine to condemn homosexuals to death amid appalling torments—as they did in parts of Western Europe in the seventeenth and eighteenth centuries."[4]

The historically prior extension of religious tolerance by members of majority creeds to minority religions and sects was itself a major advance in the story of the emergence of pluralist toleration and freedom of conscience. This point has been made emphatically: "The inclusion of religious minorities into the civil rights and political liberties was a mortal blow" to the "confessional state," to the

> direct connection between the sacred and the secular in public life.... The admission of religious minorities into the exercise of political privilege wrought profound change in Western political thought and practice. In a fundamental way, the idea of what comprises political community, and what institutions best serve its purposes, was given a new foundation.[5]

It is liberty of conscience and pluralist toleration that work against sectarian faction and the corruption of politics it engenders.

If the argument of Chapter Three is on target, that typical condemnations of homosexuality and gay persons fall into a category of morals discourse that gives expression to a religious point-of-view that is itself only tenuously, if at all, connected to a legitimate, publicly justified secular purpose, then the search is on to locate this category in relationship to constitutional jurisprudence. In this chapter we review an innovative argument against discrimination based on sexual orientation, including the ban on same-sex marriage, that derives its force from freedom of conscience and religious toleration. This argument pronounces the ban as unconstitutional under the religion clauses of the First Amendment. The First Amendment to the United States Constitution reads as follows: "Congress shall make no law respecting an establishment of religion, or prohibiting the free exercise thereof; or abridging the freedom of speech, or of the press, or the right of the people peaceably to assemble, and to petition the Government for a redress of grievances."[6]

We interpret the First Amendment's religion clauses *not* to empower the government in any way, but, rather, to deny it any legislative power to make a law that respects an establishment of religion.[7] The contribution to religious freedom made by disestablishment is not insignificant, nor has it gone unremarked:

The framers of the Constitution could not have imagined the religious diversity of America today. Nonetheless, the sturdy principles of free exercise and the nonestablishment of religion have stood the test of time. America's rich religious pluralism today is a direct result of our commitment to religious freedom. Our secular humanist traditions also are a product of the freedom of conscience built into the Constitution. Freedom of religion is also freedom from religion of any sort. . . . The twin principles of religious freedom and nonestablishment provide the guidelines for something far more valuable than a Christian or Judeo-Christian nation. They provide the guidelines for a multireligious nation . . . [8]

Richards' law review essay connects the expression in the law of a morals discourse about homosexuality, with the constitutional protections that renders it an impermissible entanglement between church and state. Richards' focus is on the denial of freedom of religious expression understood as liberty of conscience; he deduces an impermissible establishment from the denial of freedom of expression of a conscientiously-held point-of-view. In later chapters we will supplement this analytical framework with the notion of a *shadow establishment* in the law of sectarian preference that is itself unconstitutional, regardless of the rights, fundamental or otherwise, that suffer under its weight.

Richards gives the object of his essay as to:

[E]nable us better to resist the blatant political irrationalism to which these initiatives unconstitutionally pander. Much of American federal and state constitutional law, both procedural and substantive, is understood most plausibly as a way of channeling the political irrationalism the founders called faction, including prominently religious factions, through constitutional demands and structures of public reason that would detoxify its moral poisons.[9]

In the context of focusing attention on what is wrong with the recent spate of anti-gay initiatives, Richards makes the following claim that identifies the nature of the injury expressed through anti-gay legislation:

[T]he strongest constitutional argument for constitutional limits on anti-lesbian/gay right initiatives is the one that has been the least explored in the available literature and the one that all other arguments implicitly depend on for their force: namely, the initiatives in question express, through public law, constitutionally forbidden sectarian religious intolerance against the fundamental rights of conscience, speech, and association of lesbian and gay persons protected by America's first and premier civil liberty, the liberty of conscience. . . . This perspective focuses on religious intolerance as the first suspect classification under American constitutional law and the principled characterization of anti-lesbian/gay rights initiatives as reflecting this suspect classification.[10]

Richards further claims that the familiar and otherwise good arguments against anti-gay initiatives based on other approaches, such as the guarantee clause and the immutability and political powerlessness prongs of heightened scrutiny analysis, rest on an interpretive mistake and trade in mistaken analogies that provide irrelevant reasons. Richards argues that his alternative perspective clarifies and/or strengthens the arguments more familiar to us. Richards gives the motivation for his approach as follows:

> We need an approach to suspect classification analysis not burdened by these false and misleading analogies [to race and gender]. The case for the suspectness of sexual preference is stronger than any case yet made on these grounds. We need an approach that can make this case. For that approach, we must look ... to the roots of suspect classification analysis in the suspectness of religious classifications. ... and focus rather on the suspectness of the attempt to discriminate against the public claims to justice central to lesbian and gay public and private identity, on analogy to religion.[11]

When we remove from consideration the possibly permissible secular purposes often cited in defense of the ban on same-sex marriage, as we did when setting the context in the Introduction, then we see much more clearly the pure status discrimination rooted in a broadly religious framework of ideas about homosexuality, as well as the force of Richards' argument and its fit with gay persons' experience of the nature of the prejudice directed against them.[12]

The two religion clauses of the First Amendment are jointly violated by anti-gay bias in the law, because both clauses are assertions of freedom. That this violates both the Free Exercise and Establishment Clauses is in keeping with the view that the meaning of these clauses is interdependent and mutually reinforcing. An establishment may impinge on liberty, while accommodation of religious liberty may risk establishment. Freedom from any establishment whatsoever is an attribute of liberty, while freedom of religious liberty is guaranteed by disestablishment. This bias, made manifest in discrimination on grounds of sexual orientation, is, in reality, "a form of religious intolerance, a ground for suspectness older than the Equal Protection Clause itself."[13] Richards elaborates:

> The Free Exercise Clause ... thus condemns as suspect burdens placed on exercise of conscientious convictions unsupported by a compelling secular justification. And its companion, the Establishment Clause, renders suspect state support of sectarian religious views ... The state may not discriminate

either against or in favor of sectarian religious conscience, but must extend equal respect to all forms of conscience.[14]

And what has this to do with gay persons? Richards suggests, a lot:

> Lesbian and gay identity—whether irreligiously, nonreligiously, or religiously grounded—is decidedly one among these views ["the wide range of religious and irreligious views protected" by both clauses]. Such identity is grounded in critically conscientious convictions both about the empowering personal and moral good of homosexual friendship and love (grounded in the basic human good of love) and arguments of public reason about the injustice and ethical wrong of its condemnation and marginalization.[15]

Constitutional guarantees of disestablishment and free exercise are violated by anti-gay amendments that are an expression of religious intolerance through public law, in the first instance because of "the unjust sectarian degradation of the identity of lesbian and gay persons that is central to the suspectness of sexual preference.... [the] use of law to degrade lesbian and gay identity as heresy and blasphemy against true value in living."[16] Anti-gay initiatives are an expression of the political irrationalism of faction; they are political, because the active promoters of such initiatives and their anti-gay sentiment are an identifiable group arranged along a sectarian continuum. They are irrational in the perversion of constitutional principle their success embodies. Richards makes the distinctions as follows:

> All forms of conscientious conviction, whether old or new, theistic or nontheistic, are thus guaranteed equal respect on terms of a constitutional principle that renders issues of conscience morally independent of factionalized politics.... Otherwise, the mere congruence of sectarian belief among traditional religions (e.g., about the alleged unspeakable evil of homosexuality) would be ... the measure of religious liberty in particular and human and constitutional rights in general.... the measure of respect for the inalienable right of conscience.... in which a lowest common denominator of unreflective majoritarian preferences is taken to be the measure of human and constitutional rights.... the darkest nightmare of the tyrannical majority that worried America's constitutional founders.[17]

Richards, then, suggests that the invidious classification is "based on lesbian and gay personal and moral conscientious identity."[18] Richards was not the first, however, to identify this site as where the harm hits home. About three decades ago the gay liberation activist Martha Shelley discussed "branded consciousness" and the "internal violence" of the frequently self-imposed secrecy of persons who identify themselves as gay or lesbian, or attempt to evade that identification.[19]

Richards has it in mind to protect the conscientiously chosen identity of an openly gay person, one who has decided to live his or her life ethically, not in the closet. How for a gay person to live his or her life ethically, with agency, dignity, and the autonomy to make meaningful choices, is of political significance, as Richards identifies it in this passage from his recent book:

> The sacrifice of moral authenticity is not a demand any person could reasonably be asked to accept as the price for freedom from irrational prejudice, and homosexual persons can no more be reasonably asked to make such a crippling sacrifice of self than any other person.[20]

What's more, the emergence of gay persons from the realm of the "socially dead" as psychologically healthy, politically engaged selves may offer lessons to society at large regarding the ethical and civic virtues inherent in self-government, in both senses of the term.[21]

Richards suggests that the openly gay person's identity is protected on First Amendment grounds of freedom of conscience, and is violated in turn when the state imposes a sectarian normative framework through the law, which is impermissible under the same amendment. Richards writes:

> If this is a suspect classification, then the initiatives in question run afoul of our historically most robust and most textually explicit constitutional guarantees for the rights of the person.... It is time for Americans to reclaim and reaffirm their central constitutional guarantees of religious toleration and pluralism, the basic rights owed, on terms of principle, to all Americans, including lesbian and gay Americans. Nothing less than the integrity of our constitutionalism is at stake.[22]

Richards' argument is a potent one. The ban on same-sex marriage is to be taken as one manifestation in the law of a religion-based, nonsecular preference for heterosexuality; it is a point-of-view, a religiously-grounded perspective protected by the U.S. Constitution.[23] But, as with any other view, the exclusiveness imposed by legislation based in this view cannot simply be upheld for reason of a religious pedigree with which many Americans are comfortable, when it conflicts with another view that is equally protected and also a form of conscience, though fewer citizens may subscribe to it.

This is especially true here, for the view that gay and lesbian identity is unworthy of respect, rightfully despised, and deserving of injustice is just that: a view, the holding of which is protected, but not the imposing of which for reason of its alleged moral rectitude. To believe otherwise is to validate the practice of the "rankest form of unconstitutional expression of religious intolerance," "the very pith and substance of constitutionally illegitimate religious intolerance which has no proper place under the letter and spirit of American constitutionalism."[24] What's more, legislatively imposing this point-of-view may well facilitate a shrunken self-understanding by Americans of the great scope of all their rights and liberties, as Christopher Keller relates:

> Traditional moral condemnation of homosexuality has diminished the intimate, imaginative, emotional, and intellectual freedom through which homosexuals construct a personal and ethical way of life. Violence against moral and personal independence is not at the outpost of the constitutional notion of privacy an unenumerated right: it is at its very soul. It is paradoxical to mitigate the scope of unenumerated rights . . . exactly where the right would protect the moral independence of a traditionally oppressed minority.[25]

The opposing view, crowded out by a sectarian, heteronormative understanding of morality, is a conscientiously grounded, dissenting gay identity, and the opposition is between a sectarian-based restriction and a view of equal citizenship "with liberty and justice for all" subject to reasonable constraints as are publicly justified and impartially imposed. The religious point-of-view is neither (1) publicly justified, nor (2) impartially imposed, by definition. An accommodation for this view, which provides for the denial of equal rights and equal protections of some citizens' liberty interests flies in the face of sound constitutional principle, and neither is nor can be constitutionally justified.[26]

Whereas Richards' focus is on the conception of freedom of conscience grounding both religion clauses, though emphasizing the abridged liberty inherent in the second clause of the two religion clauses, the free exercise clause, our focus is on a non-preferential violation of this conception under the first clause, the establishment clause. Nonpreferentialism, customized here as the *shadow establishment,* is also establishment, whereby preference is given to religion, broadly conceived yet narrowly understood as Christian and as opposed to irreligion. Expression of this preference in the law is not a legitimate, publicly justified secular purpose.[27] The *shadow establishment* exists to the detriment of some other widely shared views, such as the conscientiously held view of many Americans that their fellow citizens who happen to be gay or lesbian are to be regarded by law in the same nonarbitrary way as are other citizens.

Discrimination based on sexual orientation, an aspect of which is the ban on same-sex marriage, is the manifestation of a perspective which is sectarian in nature. This normative perspective is what gives sense to the discriminatory intent and impact of the law as it treats gay persons, and raises the constitutional issue insofar as it infringes on a fundamental right or liberty interest. Were no one injured, and no fundamental right or liberty interest at stake, the generalized presence in the law of a religious persuasion could plausibly be construed as an appropriate accommodation to the freedom of religious expression of many Americans. But, this does not describe the situation today. Rather, for gay persons the value of liberty of conscience is less, because, as Richards has argued (1) there is a heavy restriction on, if not injury to, the exercise of equal citizenship by Americans who happen to be gay or lesbian, and (2) there is at best a conflict of rights, of protected freedoms under the general rubric of freedom of conscience. Furthermore (3) we can identify a *shadow establishment* in the law that is the root cause hampering the freedom of conscience of gay persons, manifestly through anchoring the sectarian rationale that grounds the ban on same-sex marriage.

Given those considerations, and given the fundamentality of the issue at hand—freedom to marry, marriage as a fundamental right or liberty interest—it is neither enough to say, nor accurate to say that the interests of the majority are protected in a nonobtrusive way, or that this matter is of little consequence, akin to other sufficiently secularized religious phenomena. Leonard Levy suggests that we regard the religious presence on our coinage, for example, as a trifle not worthy of judicial attention because the religious message, if any, is too trivialized and secularized to bother with.[28] With other matters, however, the perspective(s) of the putatively injured parties to the issue must be solicited. "What is trifling to the majority may be threatening and offensive, even persecuting, to a minority."[29] Of course, protected rights, fundamental freedoms and liberty interests belong to each individual American citizen, no matter how large or small their percentage of the population; they cannot be treated as trivial, without simultaneously treating the putative claimants as trivial.

The current state of the law is in fact quite the opposite of a "trifle," and is worthy of serious reexamination, as in the United States today certain of its citizens are being denied a fundamental aspect of their right to equality and protection from religious establishment in direct violation of foundational constitutional principles and doctrine. The current situation for American citizens who happen to be gay or lesbian is that they are thwarted in their liberty interest in marrying their loved one, a palpable effect indeed.

PART III

How to Identify *Sub Rosa* Establishment and the Argument by Definition

The frequently overlooked, but significant brick in the metaphorical wall of separation between church and state is the "no religious test" clause, which suggests the status of religion in the Constitution. Clause Three of Article VI of the United States Constitution states that elected public officials "both of the United States and of the several States, shall be bound by Oath or Affirmation, to support this Constitution; but no religious Test shall ever be required as a Qualification to any Office or public Trust under the United States." The deliberate nature of this minimal acknowledgment of religion is of great significance, or so one legal scholar argues:

> The only reference to religion in the original Constitution, Article VI is written in the form of an unequivocal denial of any place to be given to religious considerations in determining qualifications for public office. . . . historically without precedent. . . . at variance with the prevailing patterns and practices in all of the original colonies, and during the early years of statehood. . . . The prohibition of any religious test for public office came not only out of a religious pluralism that was rampant at the time of the nation's founding, but also out of the concept of the new Republic as a secular state. The very exclusion of any religious test for office was itself a profound acknowledgment of the secular character of the new Republic. . . . As a secular state, America is a nation in which neither religion nor irreligion enjoys any official status and where no church or religion is to enjoy any advantages or to suffer any disadvantages because of an establishment of religion. Religious identity is made irrelevant to one's rights of citizenship. . . . One's religion or irreligion may not be made the basis of political privilege or discrimination.[1]

It may be helpful to regard the question of whether an atheist can become President of the United States as a parallel issue to same-sex marriage. Here, the letter of the law regarding religion and irreligion is clear: no religious tests. The letter of the law, however, may not express *the popular view.*² *That this issue has surfaced only in relation to the candidacy of a Catholic for the Office of President may suggest that the issue is poorly specified in the abstract, and must be rendered into a denominational category in order to engage it.*

Arthur Hertzberg suggests that the United States may have an establishment after all, at a high level of Protestant abstraction such that Americans were considered free to worship the Christian God in peace and as they so chose.³ Stephen Feldman suggests that the United States displayed a de facto and thorough establishment of Protestantism at the time of the nation's Founding not because of church attendance, but because

> Protestantism and Protestant views shaped the ways that most individuals understood religion, politics, economics, and even their own individuality. . . . Perhaps the depth of Protestant hegemony was revealed less by the percentage of people attending church and more by the widespread and passionate opposition to fully accepting Jews and other non-Christians into American political life.⁴

A sectarian point of view, Hertzberg and Feldman suggest, has animated American law and politics, in the sense of what ultimately explains the good or moral rectitude in legal and policy choices that have characterized the treatment of religion generally, and what accounts for the frequently ungenerous withholding of protections, or extensions of rights and privileges where a countervailing moral issue has been discerned.

Theoretical speculation as to the constitutionality of so-called "nondenominational prayers" or "nonsectarian religious devotional exercises" is unnecessary, because at issue in any concrete case will be a real denominational preference of one sort or another, which is preempted by reading the First Amendment as erecting a wall of separation. In practice, the issue of an atheist becoming President turns on popular perception encountering explicit constitutional doctrine. This makes for one sort of shadow establishment, as it turns the Establishment Clause into a so-called nonpreferentialist statement on religion in general, rather than explicitly violating the "no religious test" clause.⁵

Constitutional silence on same-sex marriage, however, is encountered in a far less indirect way—through law's expression of a preference for religion in general, or just enough religion so as to ground the ban and give it its sense of reasonableness. Torasco made very clear, however, the Court's view of so-called nonpreferentialism, or the establishment of religion broadly conceived:

Sub Rosa *Establishment* 65

> We repeat and again reaffirm that neither a State nor the Federal Government can constitutionally force a person "to profess a belief or disbelief in any religion." Neither can constitutionally pass laws or impose requirements which aid all religions as against non-believers, and neither can aid those religions based on a belief in the existence of God as against those religions founded on different beliefs.[6]

The shadow establishment *that interests us is not nearly as explicit in the law as it was in Torasco, but exists nevertheless in the rationale for laws that ground the ban on same-sex marriage, the palpable effects of which are injurious to the personal liberty interests of a good many Americans.*

The parallel between these two shadow establishments *ends, and the real injury begins, when we realize that although there may be "no religious test" for any public office, no person has a right to become President of the United States. By contrast, every adult individual has a constitutionally protected liberty interest in the fundamental right to marry, in the personal choice of whom to marry, an interest thwarted in practice by the* shadow establishment *of sectarian preference, as the following two rulings from mixed-race marriage cases make clear:*

> Since *the right to marry is the right to join in marriage with the person of one's choice, a statute that prohibits an individual from marrying a member of a race other than his own restricts the scope his choice and thereby restricts his right to marry.* . . . *The right to marry is the right of individuals, not of racial groups.* . . . *the essence of the right to marry is freedom to join in marriage with the person of one's choice.*[7]

> *The freedom to marry has long been recognized as* one of the vital personal rights *essential to the orderly pursuit of happiness by free men.* . . . *The Fourteenth Amendment requires that* the freedom of choice to marry *not be restricted by invidious discriminations. Under our Constitution, the freedom to marry, or not marry, a person of another race* resides with the individual and cannot be infringed by the State.[8]

An alternative thesis might be that adult gay persons do not fall under the category of "individuals," but are outside it, intrinsically immoral—"anathema"—as they have been considered at various points in the history of religion and civilization in the West.[9] *A law that encodes this extreme,* per se unction *against gay persons is* prima facie *unconstitutional. So too a law that takes homosexuality itself as criminally harmful. Statutes against sodomy, an activity that presumably is* conta bonos mores, *arguably have as their real goal to place gay persons outside the relevant human community, beyond the reach of the taken-for-granted fundamental rights that all American citizens reasonably and rightfully expect.*[10]

The parallel ends, then, when we realize that, whereas no jurisdiction may decree a religious test for public office, the state can decree a ban on same-sex marriage. We have pursued the question of whether a sectarian understanding grounds this ban, establishing in the law an impermissible religious preference that grounds the injury to the status of gay Americans as equal citizens.[11] *Chapter Five follows the Court's guidance in detecting a religious preference in purportedly secular legislation. In Chapter Six we turn to the objection that same-sex marriage is an oxymoron, an innovative though ultimately sterile line of reasoning that relies on dictionary definitions to pronounce the ban on same-sex marriage constitutionally permissible, oddly, for the reason that marriage is outside the reach of the legislature. Later, in Part IV, we pursue the* shadow establishment *as that which provides the rationale for antipolygamy and miscegenation laws, as well as the ban on same-sex marriage.*

FIVE

The *Shadow Establishment* Has Its Day in Court

In the three cases we examine here, members of the Court exhumed the *shadow establishment,* and judged the permissibility of the accommodation to religious expression the statute at issue evinced. The three cases are *McCollum v. Board of Education,* 333 U.S. 203 (1948), concerning public schools' provision of release time for religious educational purposes on school grounds; *Zorach v. Clauson,* 343 U.S. 306 (1952), where the religious instruction was off-campus; and, *McGowan v. Maryland,* 366 U.S. 419 (1961), where a compulsory Sunday closing law was at issue. *McGowan*'s eight-to-one decision finding a secular purpose in Sunday Closing Laws is perhaps the strongest regarding accommodation of religion.[1] These cases were selected because they came in short succession of one another, involved pretty much the same justices, and display the Court's process of thinking through the nature of the establishment before them. In all three they found an establishment, though the statutory scheme presented to them was more or less non-preferential. The history of Establishment cases heard by the Court is long and involved; in each case our focus is limited to the reasoning used by members of the Court that helps to detect the *shadow establishment* and the grounds for its permissibility, or lack thereof.

McCollum concerned compulsory religious instruction in public schools, which was found unconstitutional under the reasoning of *Everson:* "The Constitution requires, not comprehensive identification of state with religion, but complete separation. . . . the First Amendment has erected a wall between Church and State which must be kept high and impregnable."[2] The religious instruction provided for in the statute at issue was divided into three religious groups (Protestant,

Catholic, Jewish), and pupils were released from their other public school duties in order to attend the appropriate group of their choice.

The *McCollum* Court found that "for several years there have apparently been no classes instructed in the Jewish religion."[3] Although the program of religious instruction provided for a Jewish rabbi, no doubt so as to be inclusive of the community's religious traditions, the instruction was devotional, not academic in nature. Its purpose was to educate *in* a tradition, rather than *about* a tradition. In the latter situation, academic interest in each of the three religious traditions would be encouraged so as to maintain the diversity in instruction, notwithstanding the religious breakdown of the pupils, whereas, in the former situation, educating *in* a tradition, any non-preferentialism quickly fades away.

Justice Reed, in dissent, granted the establishment at issue, but cited precedent to make the point that the "prohibition of enactments respecting the establishment of religion do not bar every friendly gesture between church and state. It is not an absolute prohibition," which is true enough.[4] Justice Reed, however, agreed that "the state cannot influence one toward religion against his will or punish him for his beliefs."[5]

Of special interest to us is Justice Frankfurter's concurring opinion, where he expounded on the principle of separation to buttress his suspicion of any dint of sectarian control in the public schools:

> Separation is a requirement to abstain from fusing functions of Government and of religious sects, *not merely to treat them all equally.* . . . Separation means separation, not something less. Jefferson's metaphor . . . speaks . . . not of a fine line easily overstepped. . . . "The great American principle of eternal separation". . . . *It is the Court's duty to enforce this principle* in its full integrity. . . . We renew our conviction that "we have staked the very existence of our country on the faith that complete separation between the state and religion is best for the state and best for religion.". . . If nowhere else, in the relation between Church and State, "good fences make good neighbors."[6]

Justice Frankfurter believed so strongly in the principle of separation that permitting even a seemingly innocuous, nonpreferentialist establishment meant that government was derelict in its duty, which importantly includes a stance towards religious sects different from the nonpreferentialist one of treating them all equally.

The principle of separation is an issue of integrity, one that gets compromised by *any* accommodation to religion, which risks the no establishment clause becoming disingenuous if the wall is not maintained, as the phrase has it, "high and impregnable." The Court's suggestion that strict separation is the government's official stance did not go unnoticed. It was in the wake of the decision in *McCollum* that some politicized members of religious communities began to organize against the "newly created crime—namely, 'secularism'. . . . It is intimated that the justices . . . are part of the conspiracy formed by 'Communists, materialists, agnostics and secularists' to wreck the freedom of education." The "judicial establishment of secularism" is "the most deadly menace to our Christian and American way of living."[7]

Opponents of the *McCollum* decision understood that Justice Frankfurter, for one, was asserting a constitutionally protected right to be free from religion, and of the state to be indifferent to religion—much in keeping with James Madison's view that religion is outside the ken of government competence to legislate.[8] Historian Irving Brant, an expert on Madison, offers these remarks on him, for whom "[r]eligion was not within the purview of the civil authority" in part because the former is outside the latter's competence. Madison, Brant goes on to say,

> looked beyond a seemingly trivial levy in aid of religious teachers, and saw its ultimate consequence in the denial of liberty and imposition of clerical control upon the state. . . . the opening given to the evils of a church establishment, and the violation of the natural and constitutional rights of the people.[9]

The decision in *McCollum* would seem to reflect Madison's line of reasoning.

The *Zorach* case also concerned religion in the schools, whereby pupils could get released from their classes to attend religious instruction elsewhere. The differences between this case and *McCollum* are twofold. In *Zorach*, pupils received instruction off the premises of the public schools, although still during the time of day when regular classes were in session, and the accommodation was upheld as constitutionally permissible. Justice Douglas delivered the opinion of the Court; the following excerpts illustrate the line of reasoning leading up to the decision:

> [O]ur problem reduces itself to whether New York by this system has either prohibited the "free exercise" of religion or has made a law "respecting an establishment of religion". . . . There cannot be the slightest doubt that the First Amendment reflects the philosophy that Church and State should be separated. The separation must be complete and unequivocal. The First Amendment within the scope of its coverage permits no exception; the prohibition is absolute. The First Amendment, however, does not say that in every and all respects there shall be a separation of Church and State. . . . there shall

be no concert or union or dependency one on the other. . . . Otherwise the state and religion would be aliens to each other—hostile, suspicious, and even unfriendly. . . . We are a religious people whose institutions presuppose a Supreme Being.[10]

Justice Douglas sees the establishment issue as one of degree, with a greater compass for accommodation than was deemed allowable under the *McCollum* decision.

Justice Douglas here articulated the nonpreferentialist position, which he acknowledged was establishment, but within permissible degrees so as to avoid showing either "partiality to any one group" or "a callous indifference to religious groups," lest "government to be hostile to religion and to throw its weight against efforts to widen the effective scope of religious influence."[11] Within the selected parameters Justice Douglas concludes:

> When the state encourages religious instruction or cooperates with religious authorities by adjusting the schedule of public events to sectarian needs, it follows the best of our traditions. *For it then respects the religious nature of our people and accommodates the public service to their spiritual needs.*[12]

Zorach, then, stands for the proposition that an establishment respecting the "religious nature" of American citizens is *not* an establishment forbidden within the meaning of the anti-establishment clause. Although no church *per se* was thereby established, a *shadow establishment* was made possible. An establishment contextualized to American religious traditions was not seen as a violation of the principle of separation; indeed, public authorities may have to make adjustments to meet the demands of sectarian groups.[13]

Justice Black, who authored the Court's opinion in *McCollum*, wrote a scathing dissent directly refuting Justice Douglas, as did Justices Frankfurter and Jackson. For Justice Black the issue was the use of state coercion to benefit religious sects:

> In considering whether a state has entered this forbidden field the question is not whether it has entered too far but whether it has entered at all. New York is manipulating its compulsory education laws to help religious sects get pupils. This is not separation but combination of Church and State.[14]

Justice Black's dissent focused attention on the victim of the *shadow establishment*, American citizens who are unbelievers; it also articulated the principle of equal citizenship under the law:

[I]t is only by wholly isolating the state from the religious sphere and compelling it to be completely neutral, that the freedom of each and every denomination and of all nonbelievers can be maintained. It is this neutrality that the Court abandons today. . . . all the more dangerous to liberty because of the Court's legal exaltation of the orthodox and its derogation of unbelievers. . . . The spiritual mind of man has thus been free to believe, disbelieve, or doubt, without repression, great or small. . . . Before today, our judicial opinions have refrained from drawing invidious distinctions between those who believe in no religion and those who do believe. The First Amendment has lost much if the religious follower and the atheist are no longer to be judicially regarded as entitled to equal justice under law.[15]

Black's dissent here echoed the concerns of his majority opinion in *Everson*: "Consequently, it [the First Amendment] cannot exclude individual Catholics, Lutherans, Mohammedans, Baptists, Jews, Methodists, Non-believers, Presbyterians, or the members of any other faith, *because of their faith, or lack of it,* from receiving the benefits of public welfare legislation."[16] Recalling Richards' links between the Establishment Clause, freedom of conscience, and gay and lesbian identity, discrimination grounded in the *shadow establishment* puts the state in the service of an invidious distinction, derogating the religious liberty of some of its citizens, those unbelievers, and benefiting some believers through an implicit grant of priority of place.

Justice Jackson in his dissent directly attended to the issue of the *shadow establishment,* which is an indirect establishment in the law of a nonpreferentialist preference for religion:

This program accomplishes that forbidden result by indirection. . . . It takes more subtlety of mind than I possess to deny that this is governmental constraint in support of religion. It is as unconstitutional, in my view, when exerted by indirection as when exercised forthrightly. . . . The day that this country ceases to be free for irreligion it will cease to be free for religion—except for the sect that can win political power.[17]

This is *sub rosa* establishment, whereby majoritarian preference for religion gets ensconced in the law *ipso facto* to the detriment of the protections of the Free Exercise Clause for unbelievers.

In the two cases examined above, *McCollum* and *Zorach,* the religious nature of the beneficiary of the law was clear. The dispute in each case concerned whether the legislation at issue in preferring religion or accommodating religious expression was thereby impermissibly establishing religion in the law. The verdict in *McCollum* turned on the issue of a government benefit to a sectarian cause, which it struck down as an impermissable entanglement. In *Zorach* the Court determined that the establishment was permissible, and so we have a *shadow establishment*. The following case, *McGowan*, is different still, in that the majority ruling took pains *not* to acknowledge the bald establishment at issue, and so not to enter the difficult terrain where arguments as to the permissibility of the accommodation are in contention. The majority opinion, however, initially did examine the establishment issue, only to reject it as inapplicable. If the majority on the Court had thought the Sunday Closing Laws were an establishment of religion, even if only broadly conceived, then they may well have struck them down as an impermissible entanglement of church and state. Instead, their move was to submerge the establishment staring them in the face, finding it too harmless and generally acceptable to merit striking it down.

In *McGowan* the issue was Sunday Closing Laws, or "blue laws," which generally prohibited the sale of goods on Sundays, and severely restricted any allowable sales.[18] This type of legislation is more burdensome to Jewish and Islamic shopkeepers than to most others, since their shops will be closed both weekend days, unless they were to renege on their religious obligations, something not asked of their Christian competitors. By contrast with *McCollum* and *Zorach,* the opinion of the Court here did not acknowledge the establishment at issue, and then proceed to either permit or not permit it. The *McGowan* Court instead found a secular purpose amidst what the layperson may be forgiven for at first glance believing is directly linked to the fourth biblical command to "obey the Sabbath." The argument is easily advanced, that the notion at work here of the days of the week being special in some way is sectarian and connected to the Biblical account of creation; hence, this notion is at its root religious and resists public, empirical confirmation or refutation.[19] There is no secular rationale that specifies one day of the week as special, since they are all alike, unless one were to respect one or other particular community's establishment of "specialness." This implies that there may be no non-arbitrary way legally to designate one day of the week as special, or to derive a civic duty to the State in honor of a special day of the week, unless as during the medieval period one were to rank the obligation to God as the mark of a good citizen, thereby respecting the establishment of religion, broadly conceived.

The opinion of the *McGowan* Court stated: "There is no dispute that the original laws which dealt with Sunday labor were motivated by religious forces."[20] The Court expressed a strong aversion on establishment grounds to uphold a law that was so motivated. However, the

Court found the Sunday Closing Laws at issue, "having undergone extensive changes from the earliest forms," no longer evince a significant sectarian purpose as had their predecessors, but, rather, are predominately secular in purpose—"presently they bear no relationship to establishment of religion as those words are used in the Constitution of the United States."[21] It was a very understandable mistake, but apparently a mistake nonetheless, to construct the case at issue as an establishment case. The course of reasoning the majority took had the following two goals, which they pursued in the face of the title of the section of the statute at issue that itself raised the establishment issue: "Sabbath Breaking."[22]

First, the majority had to eliminate the establishment issue, which they did amidst references to and quotations from *Everson* and *McCollum*, as follows:

> However, it is equally true that the "Establishment" Clause does not ban federal or state regulation of conduct whose reason or effect merely happens to coincide or harmonize with the tenets of some or all religions. In many instances, the Congress or state legislatures conclude that the general welfare of society, wholly apart from any religious considerations, demands such regulation. Thus, for temporal purposes, murder is illegal. And the fact that this agrees with the dictates of the Judeo-Christian religions while it may disagree with others does not invalidate the regulation. So too with adultery and polygamy.[23]

Secondly, the majority had to find a permissible legislative purpose within the scope of a legitimate public purpose, which they did as follows:

> The present purpose and effect of most of them [Sunday Closing Laws] is to provide a uniform day of rest for all citizens; the fact that this day is Sunday, a day of particular significance for the dominant Christian sects, does not bar the State from achieving its secular goals. To say that the states cannot prescribe Sunday as a day of rest for these purposes solely because centuries ago such laws had their genesis in religion would give a constitutional interpretation of hostility to the public welfare rather than one of mere separation of church and state.[24]

McGowan, then, was not an establishment case after all, owing to the secular, overriding legislative purpose alongside the residue of sectarian purpose.

The secular purpose of the legislation entitled "Sabbath Breaking" was restated several times by the *McGowan* Court, as in the following passages from its opinion:

These provisions, along with those which permit various sports and entertainments on Sunday, seem clearly to be fashioned for the purpose of providing a Sunday atmosphere of recreation, cheerfulness, repose and enjoyment. Coupled with the general proscription against other types of work, we believe that the air of the day is one of relaxation rather than one of religion. . . . It does talk in terms of "profan[ing] the Lord's day," but other sections permit the activities previously thought to be profane. . . . the statutes' present purpose and effect is not to aid religion but to set aside a day of rest and recreation.[25]

On this interpretation, the statute at issue seems an explicit establishment of Christian faith, broadly conceived, the purpose of which is wholly religious in nature, but with a built-in exception for non-Christians and non-believers. Questions of harm and injury to liberty interests seem out of place with such an innocent purpose and a happy effect, a day of rest, for everyone. Still, the Court had to deal with the question of why legislative purpose rested on the seventh day of the week.

The majority proffered a supplementary rationale for the statute in order to defray curiosity as to why Sunday. Sunday provides for a *uniform* day of rest: "one day apart from all others as a day of rest, repose, recreation, and tranquillity—a day in which all members of the family and community . . . a day on which people may visit friends and relatives who are not available during working days."[26] Interestingly, other sections of the statute at issue detailed which retail establishments may remain open on Sundays, selling certain goods such as tobacco products, and which could not, such as the appellants' small department store. Indeed, the statutes came to "exempt entirely any retail establishment in that County [Anne Arundel, in Maryland] which employs not more than one person other than the owner."[27] Given the looser restrictions on work activity, one can be excused for finding ever less public, secular purpose, and an attempt to regulate Sunday economic transactions differently for some other type of purpose.

In its concluding passages the opinion of the Court purports to bring to closure any doubts as to the secular purpose served through Sunday Closing Laws:

Moreover, it is common knowledge that the first day of the week has come to have special significance as a rest day in this country. People of all religions and people with no religion regard Sunday as a time for family. . . . Sunday is a day apart from all others. *The cause is irrelevant;* the fact remains. It would seem unrealistic for enforcement purposes and perhaps detrimental to the general welfare to require a State to choose a common day of rest other than that which most persons would select of their own accord.[28]

Amazingly, the Court spent considerable time persuading us of an apparent nonissue. Sunday is simply the American day of rest, and the whys and wherefores are unimportant to establishing this. Two features of the line of reasoning quoted above stand out, in addition to the emphasized passage.

First, although Sunday may be regarded as a day for family by most Americans regardless of their religion, this is not true because of a coincidence among religions on this matter. Rather, that this is true *arguendo* probably has a lot to do with the laws antecedent to the one at issue in *McGowan*.[29] Secondly, Sunday is not simply selected by people of their own accord absent some coercion through the law, but through the continuing presence of the law—here, "Sabbath Breaking"— whereby many workplaces and retail establishments are prohibited from being open for business on Sundays. The coercion falls heaviest on those whose religious beliefs have designated other days as significant, people who do not rest on Sundays, yet now may have to close shop two days a week. Those Americans of other faiths, or of no faith at all, could only wonder why "the cause was irrelevant," since only a mainstream Christian religious intereptation could have given the original and enduring choice of Sunday, the pedigree from which the non-religious social practice of "a day of rest" devolved and retains its sense.

Justice Frankfurter, in his concurring opinion, recalled the history of religious liberty in this nation, the importance of it in the colonial context, and the record of persecution by sectarian majorities. Frankfurter's unique contribution to *McGowan* was his elaboration of "this quality of interplay" between secular and religious concerns and activities.[30] To his view, so long as government presence and its effects in the overlapping areas of church and state is not subservient to sectarian creedal purpose so as to be in the service of any purely religious purpose, or religion as such, then establishment is not at issue. In the following passage Frankfurter suggests a two-pronged test:

> If the primary end achieved by a form of regulation is the affirmation or promotion of religious doctrine—primary, in the sense that all secular ends which it purportedly serves are derivative from, not wholly independent of, the advancement of religion—the regulation is beyond the power of the state. . . . Or if a statute furthers both secular and religious ends by means to the effectuation of the secular ends alone—where the same secular ends could

equally be attained by means which do not have consequences for promotion of religion—the statute cannot stand.³¹

Frankfurter's path through the wall of strict separation allowed for the Sunday Closing Laws, because their purpose was sufficiently secular in the first instance, and probably in any important sense as well, according to his perspective.

In the lone dissent, Justice Douglas asks the basic question—why Sunday, is it an especially secular day in need of special protection?—and pushes what for him is the obvious response, that only the fourth commandment—"obey the Sabbath"—makes sense of this type of law: "Sunday is a word heavily overlaid with connotations and traditions deriving from the Christian roots of our civilization that color all judgments concerning it. This is what the philosophers call "word magic."³² The Court, then, inadvertently approved an establishment in the law of something that makes sense only in the light of a certain broad, biblically based tradition's religious understanding. Thus, for Douglas the Sunday Closing Laws are a clear violation of the separation principle, its nonpreferentialism notwithstanding:

> The First Amendment commands government to have no interest in theology or ritual; it admonishes government to be interested in allowing religious freedom to flourish—whether . . . Catholics, Jews, or Protestants, or to turn the people toward . . . Buddha, or . . . Moslem nation, or to produce in the long run atheists or agnostics. On matters of this kind government must be neutral. This freedom plainly includes freedom *from* religion with the right to believe, speak, write, publish and advocate antireligious programs.³³

Douglas summed up the issue before the Court:

> The question is whether a State can impose criminal sanctions on those who, unlike the Christian majority that makes up our society, worship on a different day or do not share the religious scruples of the majority. . . . I could understand how rational men, representing a predominantly Christian civilization, might think these Sunday laws did not unreasonably interfere with anyone's free exercise and took no step toward a burdensome establishment of any religion. . . . But those who fashioned the First Amendment decided that if and when God is to be served, His service will not be motivated by coercive measures of government. . . . This means . . . that if a religious leaven is to be worked into the affairs of our people, it is to be done by individuals and groups, not by the Government.³⁴

Justice Douglas responded to the first prong of Justice Frankfurter's test by noting that the open "affirmation or promotion of religious doctrine" in Sunday Closing Laws was purposefully deleted so as not to raise the issue. Douglas cited three previous examples from case law where legislatures had made "an *ad hoc* improvisation" in the face of the "realization that the Sunday law would be more vulnerable to constitutional attack . . . if the religious motivation of the statute were more explicitly avowed."[35] Douglas' point here was invited by the majority, who found the history of the statute at issue relevant for showing its putative evolution from religious to secular. Douglas supplies the historical motive—to disguise—behind this supposed evolution from religious to secular. This putative evolution reflected a conscious effort to maintain both the blue law *and* the notion of separation of church and state "by adopting a police power rationale for Sunday legislation."[36]

As regards the second prong of Justice Frankfurter's test, Justice Douglas asks whether by fixing "a maximum hours" limitation in other terms"—such as the 40-hour workweek—the "same secular ends could equally be attained by means which do not have consequences for promotion of religion."[37] Douglas could have gone further by noting that the 40-hour workweek burdens no religious observance and infringes on no one's religious freedom, nor does it unequally place the faithful of any religion under economic pressure or threat by the criminal law.[38] Douglas' dissent implicitly confirmed the respectfulness of the strict separation principle towards the followers of all religions, as well as those American citizens who feel no respect or reverence for the Sabbath, and would rather not have public law respect its observance.

Regarding the First Amendment, Justice Douglas opined "[t]here can be in this realm no room for balancing. . . . The religious regime of every group must be respected—unless it crosses the line of criminal conduct. . . . Any other reading imports, I fear, an element common in other societies but foreign to us."[39] Finally, Douglas pronounced on the matter of Sunday Closing Laws, and asserted some disingenuousness on the part of the majority in *McGowan*:

> The Court picks and chooses language from various decisions to bolster its conclusion that these Sunday laws in the modern setting are "civil regulations." No matter how much is written, no matter what is said, the parentage of these laws is the Fourth Commandment; and they serve and satisfy the religious predispositions of our Christian communities.[40]

In *McGowan* we see the subtlety of the indirect establishment, here under the guise of secular purpose, yet without *Zorach*'s acknowledged accommodation of the religious nature of the American people as legitimating the *shadow establishment*. In *McGowan* we have none of the concerns for distinctions in the law between believers, unbelievers, and others as in *Zorach*, perhaps for reason of the *McGowan* Court's concern for maintaining the wall of separation as in *McCollum*. Because of the *McGowan* Court's concern for the separation principle it was able to hide the establishment in the law of a nonpreferentialist religious preference far more deeply than was the Court in *Zorach*. Given the significance to Christians of the seventh day of the week, Sunday, *McGowan* seems a less than nonpreferentialist establishment. This controversy in fact, and its resolution, suggests that a nonpreferentialist establishment may be incomprehensible at the level of practice, and is certainly impermissible in theory under a regime that genuinely protects freedom of conscience, understood to mean freedom from religious establishment.[41]

McGowan's Sunday Closing Laws are similar to the ban on same-sex marriage in that both have successfully hidden the sectarian rationale for their existence behind putatively legitimate governmental purpose. In both cases—Sunday closing laws, the ban on same-sex marriage—what gives the outcome its sense is to understand it as expressing a morals preference in the law that is sectarian in nature. Many Americans have agreed with Madison regarding the competence of the government in the area of religion; we would do well to question the State's competence in the area of regulating interpersonal relationships such as the eligibility of adults to marry their beloved. Understanding the religion clauses to work in tandem, an establishment in the law of one religion's understanding of one day of the week as a special day is an infringement on others' freedom of religious expression. So too is establishing in the law one religion's understanding of the institution of marriage an infringement on others' liberty interest and right to marry.

The *shadow establishment*, then, is not a state church or preference for any or all churches, but for religion broadly conceived, nonpreferentially understood, and indirectly established under a likely sham secular rubric. But, there's one big difference between the *shadow establishment* in *McGowan* and that in the ban on same-sex marriage: the absence of secular purpose in the latter, which is not an option. We do not have to pass judgment on the *McGowan* Court's accommodation of religion, or on the tightness of the connections between sectarian and secular purposes, to assert the ban's unique characteristic in this regard.[42] Put differently, the notion of the *shadow establishment*, a First

Amendment violation, provides a lens to identify those accepted and assumed lawful practices that burden the enjoyment of fundamental rights and liberties by some American citizens, ultimately for reason of a still-present sectarian bias in the law, without the saving grace of a legitimate public secular purpose.

SIX

A Note Regarding the Appeal to the Dictionary

The discussions in Chapters Four and Five that reveal the contours of the *shadow establishment* have direct bearing on the argument by definition often used by opponents of same-sex marriage. At first glance the argument by shift from constitutional issue to linguistics appears transparent and unworthy of consideration; however, its unsuspecting innocence has given it a powerful role in several court cases.[1] This line of reasoning, restricting the extent of the right to marry to a dictionary definition of marriage, is question-begging, suggesting as it does that *American Heritage* or *Webster's* are the nation's foundational documents.

Here, the move is to sidestep the difficulties inherent in defending discrimination based on sexual orientation on the grounds of majoritarian preference, which runs the risk of undermining its legitimacy, while suggesting that no perspective at all is at work here, save for the law's impartial rendering of simple dictionary definitions. This move invites argumentation by circular reasoning, because (1) the dictionary definition was put there by some person(s) through some process of interpretation based on one or other aspect(s) of usage; (2) most likely no constitutional filter was in place anywhere in the process; so that (3) the dictionary definition may simply and unreflectively manifest the issue at hand, an issue of heteronormative bias masquerading as an unobjectionable item of innocuous discourse.[2] That is to say, the definition one finds in the dictionary may already be the product of bias and distortion, and appealing to it answers nothing important, although it serves rhetorically to ground the pose of impartiality and to leave the legislative choice unremarked. One legal scholar with prominent contributions on the topic of same-sex marriage ably communicates the latter point:

The importance of the difference between a legislature's choosing not to recognize same-sex marriages and the legislature's being precluded from recognizing same-sex marriages has not been appreciated. The legal analysis of the relevant issues is very different if the nonrecognition is a legislative choice rather than something that would be ultra vires for the legislature to change. . . . Where the state itself is the entity defining the relevant term, the definition must be viewed in the same way that any other legislative classification would be viewed—to be valid, it must be reasonably related to the promotion of a legitimate goal. Legislatures cannot avoid having their statutes subject to judicial review simply by using definitions to accomplish their legislative aims.[3]

Dictionary definitions are to some extent products of society that reflect at least a partial consensus at one point in time that is nonetheless open to challenge and, possibly, redefinition, even in an area as seemingly stable and familiar as human sexuality.[4] What's more, definitions in statute law are entirely the product of the legislative body, and can be changed at its whim. Still, this tactic is powerful because it appears that no bias is operative—that the legislature's hands are tied, that even the Court must bow to the dictionary as it represents the way things are. Dictionary definitions are descriptive, not normative, although these two may get conflated in a particular word, the true meaning of which may be so entirely embedded in a religious tradition such that it is by definition normative—"sabbath," perhaps.[5] The *shadow establishment*, by definition, would describe in neutral terms what is meaningful only in the context of an historical sectarian tradition, appeal to which is a dubious move when the presence of the tradition in the civil law is itself at issue.

Waiting for dictionary definitions to change based on society's continually evolving understanding hides law's role in inhibiting that conceptual evolution, that enlarged social understanding of a word in use, in its context. This role points to another reason why this is a circular argument that carries no weight even definitionally, much less constitutionally. The utility of this tactic of appealing to black-and-white dictionary definitions may be foreclosed in due course regardless.[6] Not realizing the continually evolving character of marriage, and that other types of marriage are conceivable and in practice elsewhere, opponents mistakenly assume that the definition of marriage is limited *per se*.[7]

Debates as to the law are settled by reference to the United States Constitution and authoritative interpretations, not by reference to a dictionary. After all, how are terms such as "abomination unto," "taboo," or "anathema" to be rendered into constitutional jurisprudence, much less pass constitutional muster regarding the rights of American citizens who happen to be gay or lesbian? Supporters of a gay couple's right to marry could rely on dictionary definitions to strike down as an impermissible entanglement any law that seeks to inscribe a taboo as such, which is inseparable from its tribal religious context, or what is considered abomination unto or anathema, which are inseparable from biblical connotations.[8] Each of these words frequently appears in connection with legislation and courtroom discussion of homosexuality and so gay persons, as in the following example:

> The state statute in question . . . forbids and condemns the practice of sodomy. Sodomy is an act upon or concerning the physical being of a person. It is an act of immemorial *anathema* both at common law, wherein it was punishable by death . . . and in ancient times. Genesis 19: 1–29. It is clearly an offense involving moral turpitude whether defined by common law or by statute.[9]

In another sodomy case, the Court found the statute at issue sensible given its distinguished parentage: "[T]he longevity of the Virginia statute does testify to the State's interest and its legitimacy. It is not an upstart notion; it has ancestry going back to Judaic and Christian law." At which point a footnote reference was made to the biblical book Leviticus 18:22, and the immemorial passage was quoted: "Thou shalt not lie with mankind, as with womankind: it is *abomination*."[10] Political theorist Jacqueline Stevens argues that the discursive supremacy of religion works its worst hardships in the areas of gender and sexual orientation, through the frequent use of a familiar, biblically-rooted morals vocabulary that locates and punishes persons who fall into either or both of these categories.[11]

The moral and legal significance of the concept of sexual orientation is socially constructed, and need not facilitate or foreclose access to the institution of marriage.[12] Even if one does not accept wholesale the theoretical notion of heteronormativity, which we have identified as a sectarian morals perspective that is present in the law, heterosexuality itself is supposed to be a distinctive sexual orientation with its own valences that some have taken to be of normative significance *simpliciter*, worthy of constitutional protection. As such, definitions that devolve from heterosexual assumptions are suspect for their neutrality; chances are good they evince an invidious distinction.[13] The real issue is not whether the law accords well with dictionary definitions, but, rather, the availability of the institution of marriage and the fit of same-sex couples to it, given any legitimate public purpose that can be considered the proper objects of the government's blessings through secular, nonarbitrary legislation.

Given Richards' thesis regarding impermissible establishment marked by infringement of the liberty of conscience, as well as the recent move simply to apply one current definition of marriage to the law, it is a point of extreme irony to note members of the clergy in several denominations arguing against the ban on same-sex marriage on the First Amendment grounds of no establishment and free expression. These religious figures, who are licensed and approved by the state to solemnize marriages, to marry individuals as per their religious traditions, have had their marriages, or "holy unions," of gay and lesbian couples declared invalid, not a real marriage by definition.[14] They counter argue that it is they, in the framework of their religious tradition, not the state, who set the definition, and that the dominion of those less progressive of their clerical brethren should not be allowed to inhibit them from doing so. In these contemporary Christian denominations, a same-sex union conforms to the sacra-mentality of two human beings' expression of one another as is meant by "marriage."[15] These clergy perceive the *shadow establishment,* and propose that the state ought to be committed to neutrality among adult couples in this regard, and to equality as regards the different marriages within their conception. Never was it truer that politics makes strange bedfellows![16]

One route out of this definitional quandary would be to let individual couples decide for themselves within their communities of faith, or otherwise, what marriage signifies for them and their communities, rather than have a definition imposed on them by the State. This approach is in keeping with libertarian tenets, as Boaz relates:

> Libertarians don't think the government needs to support and encourage traditional families, as moralistic conservatives advocate. It just needs to stop undermining families so people can form the kinds of families they want. Ideally ... [it] should get out of the marriage and family business altogether. ... It is wrong to deny same-sex couples the right to marry today. ... There's also the basic human dignity of being able to make a public affirmation of one's love and commitment. ... It's hard to see how the acceptance of same-sex marriages would undermine anyone else's marriage. ... And surely *more* people getting married is good for the institution of marriage.[17]

The libertarian challenge to the nation's marriage laws, then, is either to eliminate any discrimination that affects couples' eligibility to marry, or to cease regulatory involvement with the marriage relationship and pursue its secular interests in, for example, a stable family life for children, and clear guidelines for divorce, adoption, and inheritance, through other means. Changing the nation's anachronistic marriage laws so as better to reflect the evolving understanding of marriage would be to treat it as any other social and legal institution, no other of which is legally frozen to exclude certain American citizens who are socially eligible for legal inclusion and the extension of associated benefits and burdens.

∽

In Part IV we review the sectarian nature of the dispute regarding state regulation of marriage, and reveal the constitutional infirmity grounded in its nonpreferentialism, one of the signature *indicia* of the *shadow establishment*. Fortunately, there are ways to coax the establishment out of the shadows, because here the secular purpose is highly tenuous for reason of the prominent use of morals discourse by the Court to justify forbidding different types of marriage, to which we now turn.

PART IV

The *Shadow Establishment*, "Gay Marriage" in the Courts, and the Analogies to Race and Polygamy

The constitution of the family organization, which is founded in the divine ordinance, as well as in the nature of things, indicates the domestic sphere as that which properly belongs to the domain and functions of womanhood. . . . The paramount destiny and mission of woman are to fulfill the noble and benign offices of wife and mother. This is the law of the Creator. And the rules of civil society must be adapted to the general constitution of things, and cannot be based upon exceptional cases. . . . In the nature of things it is not every citizen of every age, sex, and condition that is qualified for every calling and position.[1]

The religious nature of the rationale for separating the spheres of men and women is made clear in the 1873 case from which the above quotation was taken. Indeed, under **Bradwell**, the state is under an obligation to comport its laws to that higher law, taken as the best expression of the way things are in the universe of facts and values. Although such an approach may well suit a lawyerly medieval scholastic, it is emphatically **not** the way of American constitutionalism with its bars to the establishment of religion and its commitment to equal protection of the laws in a republic of limited government. Unfortunately, **Bradwell**-type rulings have been all too common in the area of marriage regulation, a trend that continues to this day in the ban on same-sex marriage.

Rather than look for similarities across the categories of being gay or lesbian and being Black or a polygamist, we will examine the similarities in the nature of the discrimination presented, the source of the discriminatory intent, and the rationale given to justify the discrimination based on race, marital regime, or sexual orientation. We *present the strength of the analogy we make across the categories as resting on the commonality in the nature of the discrimination, specifically, its originating sectarian rationale, rather than on an argument that purports to demonstrate that Black and gay American citizens, for example, are similarly situated* a priori *of their legal context. The court cases are discussed with a concern for detecting an impermissible expression of sectarian bias in the law—the* shadow establishment—*identified when the rationale and source of the marriage legislation at issue are ultimately religious in nature, as we will see the Court on occasion explicitly acknowledge under the cloak of legitimate public purpose. We find that understanding marriage discrimination to be based on sectarian preference better assesses the situation than does the analogy to anti-polygamy, itself a better analogy than the analogy to anti-miscegnation, because of the religious preference at work in each.*

As discussed in the introduction to Part III, it has been the case in the American context, that "Protestantism is, in effect, the culture religion of the United States. . . . a kind of chaplaincy to the status quo" that, in matters of sexuality, both grounds and is grounded in heterosexism.[2] *Our argument is that understanding the ban on same-sex marriage, as well as prohibitions against interracial and plural marriages, as sectarian-inspired provides the best explanation of the sense these bans' supporters have had of the goodness or rightfulness of this type of legislation. The Judeo-Christian tradition may perhaps still provide a majority of Americans with their sense of beginnings and belonging in an ultimate sense; the legitimacy of this private view is not our focus here, just any impermissible validation of it in public law. The term "Judeo-Christian" is frequently applied to describe traditional American morality, as well as its social roots. Nevertheless, the hyphenated entity "Judeo-Christian" is a misnomer instantly recognizable by anyone familiar with the history of the two great traditions' interactions, or their truly distinctive self-interpretations.*[3] *The Judeo-Christian linkage is at so high a level of abstraction that one barely, if at all, notices the fundamental theological differences thereby occluded from view, differences which in practice have at times bode for the worse for American Jews.*

The court cases discussed in the two chapters that follow represent a focused, not comprehensive, treatment of the lay of the land as regards marital regimes in the United States. With each innovation in the marriage relationship, and each new difference in its practice and the parties to it, there has been a reaction suggesting that "marriage" is in decline, about to surrender or be overtaken by something less worthy or un-American. The threatened Mormon innovation, for example, was met with defensive maneuvers designed, bluntly rather than artfully, to protect an understanding of the institution of marriage that combined religion, monogamy, and sexuality, as Mormon scholar B. Carmon Hardy relates:

> The Republican Party's well-known 1856 pledge to rid the country of "those twin relics of barbarism—polygamy and slavery" was an oath salted through with sexual implication. . . . The danger presented an especially threatening countenance because Mormon polygamy emerged in the national consciousness just as monogamy was acquiring status not only as preferred but as a vital prerequisite of Western civilization. . . . concern lay less with the sexual derelictions of individuals than a sense that the form of the monogamous home was threatened. The purpose of anti-polygamy laws was to expunge the "semblance" of a competing, non-monogamic order of home life.[4]

The reality is that the Republic has endured the feared changes rather well, with the institution of marriage finding itself strengthened, or at least more in demand, for reason of its being tailored to meet the needs of an ever more inclusive American society.[5] The analogies to laws against interracial and polygamous marriage, we argue below, betray an underlying morals regime and sectarian rationale that do not befit American ideals of equal citizenship and equal protection of the laws for all, with the suggestion being, so too the ban on same-sex marriage.

SEVEN

Interracial and Plural Marriage Analogies and Cases

The Miscegenation Analogy

This analogy, which suggests that the bar to marriage for gay persons is analogous to the bar to interracial marriage, is a topic well-covered in the literature.[1] Two book-length treatments of this topic reward consultation. Robert J. Sickels discusses the miscegenation taboo and links it to a dread of homosexuality; additionally, he suggests that the power of this taboo is properly understood to reside in the realm of sexuality, though alongside a caste system inextricably based in race.[2] More recently, Rachel F. Moran has discussed anti-miscegenation laws in terms of perpetuating a regime of caste that catches white people in its grip as well, and is effected by law through inscribing different valences to different interpersonal relationships between citizens, to the detriment of individual equality.[3]

Statutes that forbade interracial marriages nearly always meant the marriage between a Caucasian or white person, and a non-white person, usually an African or person of African descent, or an Asian "oriental."[4] Frequently, such laws also referred to Native American Indians as well as persons of Hispanic descent.[5] Laws against interracial marriage and family relations, especially as regards Blacks and Asians, were "a hallmark of intense racialization and entrenched unequality."[6] Our discussion will embellish Sunstein's conception of the Equal Protection Clause of the U.S. Constitution as an "anti-caste principle," with the analogy to miscegenation suggesting that the ban on same-sex marriage also works to create a "caste" within the American citizenry, which is nearly inevitable whenever equal protection is violated.[7] This to say, the sort of reasoning that keeps the ban in place is identical to one that seeks to carve out a (lower) caste of persons in American society. Andrew Koppelman views the legal regime of anti-miscegenation in a similar way:

> My claim is that the taboo against homosexuality is not irrational but serves a function similar to that of the taboo against miscegenation. Both taboos police the boundary that separates the dominant from the dominated in a social hierarchy that rests on a condition of birth. In the same way that the prohibition of miscegenation preserved the polarities of race on which white supremacy rested, the prohibition of homosexuality preserves the polarities of gender on which rests the subordination of women.[8]

Richards has supplied us with a deeper understanding of the grounding of the comparable prohibitions against same-sex marriage: the reasoning is sectarian; its result is a caste of persons who too count as "3/5" citizens.

The State of Virginia boldly asserted its sectarian reasoning in its famous defense of its anti-miscegenation statutory scheme: "Almighty God created the races white, black, yellow, malay and red, and he placed them on separate continents. . . . The fact that he separated the races shows that he did not intend for the races to mix."[9] Interestingly, the State of Virginia's anti-miscegenation statute included an exception for descendants of Virginia's mythical-historical First Family—John Rolfe and Pocahontas. Exceptions in law and practice to supposedly principled taboos against interracial relationships might in fact more reflect other traditional aspects of marriage law, such as securing lands for one or other faith, promotion of military alliances, and political ambitions involving power and wealth.[10]

In the two other most frequently cited miscegenation cases, the sectarian reasoning in support of the statute at issue was also made clear. In *McLaughlin v. Florida* (379 U.S. 184 [1964]), a precursor to *Loving*, the statute expressed its concerns for promiscuity, "lewd and lascivious behavior," and "sexual decency," in traditional morals discourse with the impermissible racial overlay. In the earlier case of *Perez v. Lippold* (198 P.2d 17 [California] [1948]), the antimiscegenation laws at issue were defended in the dissenting opinion, where Justice Shenk dodged the charges of ignorance and prejudice, and pointed to a higher calling:

> It will also be shown that they have a valid legislative purpose even though they may not conform to the sociogenetic views of some people. . . . to impose such restraints upon the [marriage] relation as the laws of God, and the

laws of propriety, morality and social order demand. . . . If any provision of that instrument [the U.S. Constitution] confers upon a citizen the right to marry any one who is willing to wed him, our attention has not been called to it. . . . The amalgamation of the races is not only unnatural, but is always productive of deplorable results.[11]

The religious aspect to the anti-miscegenation regime drew one reviewer to comment on "the presence in American society and law of a remarkable symbiosis between widely shared sacred and secular views on marriage."[12] The same reviewer opined that the "ringing words of the Court" in *Loving* regarding the freedom to marry as no longer "successfully separated from the freedom to marry the person of one's choice," will long after this decision "continue to have an impact of enormous significance."[13] This point was picked up in a law review essay about ten years later:

> The disinclination of the Court to extend *Loving*-type protections beyond the heterosexual and monogamous context suggests that the Court fears extension of constitutional protection to bizarre lifestyle choices would threaten traditional American conceptions of family life. So great, in fact, is our emotional investment in orthodox family life that the rationality of these fears and the reality of the threat may never be fully tested. The final irony of *Loving* is thus laid bare.[14]

The irony of which the authors just quoted may be unaware is that *Loving* overturned one "traditional American conception of family life," while another one similarly is being tested in the first instance for reason of its being orthodox, and for the quality of rationality relied on publicly to support it.

Another commentator has also misconstrued the holding in *Loving*, here, to concern an issue of opposite-sex rights, rather than one of an individual's rights that were being abridged on account of his race. Richard F. Duncan, an arch opponent of same-sex marriage, advances an argument based in "moral discernment":

> Because race is irrelevant to what makes a relationship a marriage, it was immoral and unconstitutional for Virginia to forbid interracial marriages. However, unlike Virginia's racist restriction on marriage, the dual-gender requirement is based upon the inherent sexual complementarity of husband and wife. . . . The dual-gender requirement, like the decision in Loving, is animated by a moral sense that discerns the true nature of marriage. . . . The legacy of Loving is dishonored by those who seek to use it as a tool to radically remake the institution of marriage . . .[15]

Duncan believes that to deny the "dual-gender requirement" is to fail at moral discernment, which one would exercise through discrimination on the basis of sexual orientation. This betokens a heteronormative understanding of both the institution of marriage and sexual orientation, the sense of which is unavailable outside a world view that is sectarian and self-validating, and inappropriately rendered into law in the American context. The irony which Duncan apparently wishes to occlude is that, as he writes, just as "Loving not only renounced the poisonous doctrine of White Supremacy, it also freed the institution of marriage from the debasement of anti-miscegenation laws," the fencing out of American citizens who happen to be gay or lesbian from marrying the loved one of their choice signifies just as clearly a "poisonous doctrine" or "debasement," of heterosexism, at least in the eyes of a growing number of people of goodwill.[16] Duncan, like not a few conservative moralists, may both reject racism as unacceptable, and yet embrace heterosexism as an appropriate moral outlook in American society, seeing the former, but not the latter, as drawing an invidious distinction.

Contrary to Duncan, however, a distinction drawn on sexual orientation is perceived as less legitimate today than was a racial classification at the time of the ruling in *Loving*, with neither distinction able to hold any ground were it not for the religious dimension hiding inside it, retaining for both classifications a measure of goodness where otherwise a neutral observer might see only the injury of discrimination and attribute it to an unfiltered, naked personal or group preference. In both cases, that of anti-miscegenation laws and the ban on same-sex marriage, the effect is to limit the formation of certain diverse communities in the United States in the service of an ultimately sectarian-grounded purpose, one either racist or heterosexist. The limitation is effected through denying to certain adult individuals their choice in whom to marry, which, in the final analysis, restricts their personal autonomy and ability to act as equal citizens.[17] Although it is true that during the twentieth century explicitly racist sectarian arguments were eclipsed by secular rationales, the underlying racism, vouchsafed by religion, nonetheless imparted its spirited animus to science.[18] The result was that the move to ground anti-miscegenation statutes in science was motivated by a need to find a cover for an obviously unconstitutional purpose, one similar to the move in *McGowan* to drape secular purpose over impermissibly religious legislation.

The Polygamy Analogy

Polygamy is the form of plural marriage commonly associated with Mormonism in the United States, the focus of this section, though the Mormon practice of one man with two or more wives is technically known as "polygyny." Plural marriage was practiced in Judaism into the Middle Ages, and is also practiced by some Muslims, Hindus, and African tribes, as well as some native peoples.[19] Mormons are often stereotyped, rather than understood with either charity or reason.[20] The cases in this section would seem to present a clear conflict of religious expression, where one sectarian view is favored over another.[21] The means to this favor were asserted *sub silentio* in the process of asserting civil authority over marriage regulation, as opposed to religious authority such as the Mormon Church presented and thought protected by the Free Exercise Clause:

> So here, as a law of the organization of society under the exclusive dominion of the United States, it is provided that plural marriages shall not be allowed. Can a man excuse his practices to the contrary because of his religious belief? To permit this would be to make the professed doctrines of religious belief superior to the law of the land, and in effect to permit every citizen to become a law unto himself. Government would exist in name only under such circumstances.[22]

Yet, why is the civil authority against polygamy? Herein lies our interest, and herein we shall find the *shadow establishment*. The Court in *Reynolds* illuminates this issue:

> Polygamy has always been odious among the Northern and Western Nations of Europe and, until the establishment of the Mormon Church, was almost exclusively a feature of the life of Asiatic and African people.... from the earliest history of England polygamy has been treated as an offense against society.... there has never been a time in any State of the Union when polygamy has not been an offense against society.... Marriage, while from its very nature a sacred obligation, is, nevertheless in most civilized nations, a civil contract, and usually regulated by law.... unless restricted by some form of constitution, it is within the legitimate scope of the power of every civil government to determine whether polygamy or monogamy shall be the law of social life under its dominion.[23]

Reynolds teaches us that marriage is inherently a "sacred obligation"; the state must choose one marital regime to support, and is justified in choosing monogamy. Apparently, as with opposite-sex marriage, the existence of one marital regime requires that no others be allowed, possibly to be granted legitimacy. Yet, why not polygamy, especially given its basis in the Old Testament, with its polygamous patriarchs, and in the mosaic tradition, not to mention its deeply held significance for members of the Mormon Church?[24] That the state can regulate the marriage relationship does not answer this query, or give sense to any particular policy.

In the later case of *Murphy v. Ramsey* (29 L.Ed. 47 [1884]), at issue were Acts governing the Utah Territory issued against bigamy and polygamy, and disenfranchising anyone who bore the status of being a bigamist or a polygamist. Again, the Court expressed the sovereignty of the national government, and elaborated as follows the rationale used to justify its stance against bigamy and polygamy:

> For certainly no legislation can be supposed more wholesome and necessary in the founding of a free, self-governing commonwealth, fit to take rank as one of the co-ordinate States of the Union, than that which seeks to establish it on the basis of the idea of the family, as constituting in and springing from the union for life of one man and one woman in the holy estate of matrimony; the sure foundation of all that is stable and noble in our civilization, the best guaranty of that reverent morality which is the source of all beneficent progress in social and political improvement.[25]

The *Murphy* Court was not concerned with establishment violations, and so was freer than was the Court in *Reynolds* to identify the civil authority with "reverent morality" as the good vouchsafed in the final analysis by anti-polygamy laws. Realizing the "holy estate of matrimony" was the purpose of the anti-polygamy laws.

The next case we consider, *Davis v. Beason* (33 L.Ed. 637 [1890]), also involved requiring Mormons to register to exercise the right to vote or to hold political office, in Idaho, and included a lengthy discussion of the First Amendment. The *Davis* Court was still less restrained than either of the earlier Courts, thusly exposing to a greater view the *shadow establishment:*

> And on this point there can be no serious discussion or difference of opinion. Bigamy and polygamy are crimes by the laws of all civilized and Christian countries.... They tend to destroy the purity of the marriage relation, to disturb the peace of families, to degrade women and to debase men. Few crimes are more pernicious to the best interests of society and receive more general or deserved punishment. To extend exemption for such crimes would be to shock the moral judgment of the community. To call their advocacy a tenet of religion is to offend the common sense of mankind.... Probably never before

in the history of this country has it been seriously contended that the whole punitive power of the government, for acts recognized by the general consent of the Christian world in modern times as proper matters for prohibitory legislation, must be suspended in order that the tenets of a religious sect encouraging crime may be carried out without hindrance.[26]

The Court in *Davis* refrained from applying the religious principle of toleration, and revealed the Christian bias ensconced in the law that links the punitive power of government to Christianity. The *Davis* Court's Devlin-like rendition would have infuriated John Stuart Mill, who had strained to understand what is the issue in the following pertinent passage from Chapter IV of his essay *On Liberty:*

The article of the Mormonite doctrine which is the chief provocative to the antipathy which thus breaks through the ordinary restraints of religious tolerance, is its sanction of polygamy; which, though permitted to Mahomedans, and Hindoos, and Chinese, seems to excite unquenchable animosity when practiced by persons who speak English and profess to be a kind of Christians.[27]

The last nineteenth-century case we examine lacked even *Davis'* minimal restraint, and made visible the *shadow establishment* as that which supplies the rationale that makes understandable the laws at issue. Here, the *shadow establishment* undergirds the Court's reasoning whereby the dissolution of the Mormon Church and the transfer of much of its property to the United States government was upheld:

But it is also stated in the findings of fact, and is a matter of public notoriety, that the religious and charitable uses intended to be subserved and promoted are the ... doctrines of the Mormon Church ... one of the distinguishing features of which is the practice of polygamy—a crime against the laws, and abhorrent to the sentiments and feelings of the civilized world.... a blot on our civilization.... a return to barbarism. It is contrary to the spirit of Christianity and of the civilization which Christianity has produced in the Western World. ... The tale is one of patience on the part of the American government and people, and of contempt of authority and resistance to law on the part of the Mormons. Whatever persecutions they may have suffered in the early part of their history ... they have no excuse.... The state has a perfect right to prohibit polygamy, and all other open offenses against the enlightened sentiment of mankind, notwithstanding the pretense of religious conviction.... *The principles of the law of charities are not confined to a particular people or nation, but prevail in all civilized countries pervaded by the spirit of Christianity.*[28]

Although the above-quoted passages contain an admirable, concessionary acknowledgment, relatively speaking, of the fact that the Mormons relocated outside the boundaries of the proper United States so as to live in peace according to their religious dictates, the "spirit of Christianity" nonetheless reached thereunto, and under its cover the civil authority of the United States. Conformity in the law to traditional American religious views, not a legitimate secular interest for its own sake, was one effect of the polygamy cases. Gay persons who wish to marry are similarly constricted.

In the twentieth century, courts have been fairer to the Mormons and those of them who practice plural marriage, but stopping short of validating polygamous marriage and continuing to use a morals discourse invoking a mildly Christian civilization.[29] For example, in a recent case involving the adoption of children by a family organized by a plural marriage, the Supreme Court of Utah perceived the conflict between the morality upheld earlier by the trial court, and constitutional requirements of fairness to all citizens:

> The result of the trial court's dismissal of this petition is to engraft upon the statute a type of "public policy" requirement that prohibits certain kinds of "wrongdoers" from judicial review of the merits of their petitions for adoption.... The fact that our constitution requires the state to prohibit polygamy does not necessarily mean that the state must deny any or all civil rights and privileges to polygamists.[30]

A final aspect of the analogy between the ban on same-sex marriage and that against plural marriage is the idea that if the heteronormative cocoon is cracked to allow for the one, it will be but a matter of a little time and the other will follow in its train, with other, "kinky" practices, now illegal, thereafter being decriminalized as well.[31] The problem here is that at work on both sides of the slippery-slope aspect to the analogy is a view of human agency that is arguably incompatible with a liberal-democratic regime.[32]

The Mormon plural marriage regime, one might argue, is based on a shared community ethos that sublimates any individual's conception or interest, and is taken to be an individual's true interest. By contrast, the expansion or redefinition of the institution of marriage legally to include same-sex couples is very much in keeping with America's liberal-democratic ethos, which not only grants to the adult individual, but also protects her in a wide range of free choice in the conduct of personal life, including a liberty interest in marrying the loved one of her choice.[33] If the concern is genuine, that prohibiting same-sex marriage is the means also to prohibit plural marriage, it is misguided. Alternatively, this concern, as a basis for legitimating the ban on same-sex marriage, might be more what it appears at first blush to be: an attempt to cover a wide reservoir of antipathy towards homosexuality, gay persons, and, probably too, Mormon adherents of the goodness of plural marriage. In actuality, then, the ban directs its most potent enmity towards gay and lesbian persons through non-recognition of the love relationships that are taken to characterize them as persons, and to distinguish them from opposite-sex couples who seek to marry.

EIGHT

"Gay Marriage" in the Courts

In this final chapter we present the morals discourse and argument by definition that supply the rationale for denying the right to marry to same-sex couples in the few cases this has arisen. Were the ban on same-sex marriage not held in place by the *shadow establishment,* it would fall for lack of secular purpose, much as would a Sunday Closing Law absent the religious history because it would not then make sense, provided any of this sort of legislation rests on its merits. There is good reason for believing that the sense of this type of legislation does indeed rest on its merits, and is well understood by its supporters, just as they also well understand the need not to advocate explicitly on those merits. In the case of same-sex marriage, however, the actual merit of the ban presents constitutional infirmities. It does not reflect a sound public policy rationale or purpose, once uncovered. In addition, the ban is a curiously unfit tool that mistakes the form of a marriage for its substance, and so does not even achieve its goal of protecting a traditional, sectarian understanding of marriage. Were its advocates more forthright, they would scrutinize individual marriages more carefully, invoking State power far more often than popular understanding of the ban would suggest. Advocates of the ban, then, present a sectarian challenge not only to change in the estate of matrimony, but also to the liberal-democratic values of the American constitutional regime, which importantly includes the protection of individual rights and liberties and a commitment to public discourse.

Same-sex marriage should be distinguished from "gay marriage." A same-sex marriage involves two individuals of the same sex or gender, who are the beloved of each other. A "gay marriage" need only involve two individuals who are gay or lesbian, including a marriage involving one of each.[1] The court in *Baehr* enunciated this general notion as a consequence of determining that the sexual orientation of the parties to a marriage is irrelevant to the granting of a marriage license: "Homosexual" and "same-sex" marriages are not synonymous; by the same token, a "heterosexual" same-sex marriage is, in theory, not oxymoronic. . . . Parties to a same-sex marriage could theoretically be either homosexuals or heterosexuals."[2]

Starting in the mid-nineteenth century and up to the gay rights movement that began in the early 1950s, these "gay marriages" were convenient for the gay persons involved because entering into this institution cast aside societal doubt about their sexual orientation.[3] Gay men and lesbians would marry one another to achieve a modicum of safety in a society roundly hostile towards them, and, in conjunction with other similarly married couples, to enjoy a secure family life closer to their choosing without tipping outsiders of their true, "deviant" identities.[4] As with not a few traditional, heterosexual marriages of convenience, the gay persons in these marriages were not erotically attracted to one another, and formed erotic, sexual attachments, sometimes long-term, with same-sex partners obviously outside the marriages; moreover, the gay persons in these marriages did not form marital bonds that surpassed friendships. Given the traditional sense of marriage that many today feel is being threatened by same-sex marriage, who also would have the law reflect and enforce their understanding, should not these alternative opposite-sex marriages have been illegal?

The question arises: is a married couple consisting of one gay or bisexual man and one lesbian or bisexual woman a marriage in the sense advocates of traditional heterosexual marriage arrangements have in mind and seek to protect in the law, such as through the Defense of Marriage Act? While the form of an opposite-sex married couple is present, this alternative pair certainly lacks the substance, even if any particular couple chose to have a child. Just as with their heterosexual counterparts, many gay men and lesbians desire to have children, and many do not, indicating that the desire to procreate and sexual orientation do not map out onto one another.

If advocates of traditional, exclusively heterosexual marriages genuinely seek to maintain both the form and substance of the institution, then they should also ban pairings that lack one *or* the other. Same-sex marriages evince the substance, though not the form; "gay marriages" include those in form only. Just as anti-same-sex sodomy statutes that went unenforced—though it was deemed vital that they remain on the books—had as their real target the marking out of certain persons in the law, so too does the ban on same-sex marriage have as its real target the enforcement of a moral disapprobation on certain persons.[5] But, unlike the insult of sodomy laws that could be avoided with discretion, if not outright ignored, the ban on same-sex marriage works an even more vicious path across American society, affecting not same-sex couples so much as gay persons individually. This is a status discrimination resting on constitutionally suspect and, as we have argued so far in this chapter, dubious grounds. Below we briefly review some cases involving same-sex marriage in the courts, cases rife with religious bromide.

In *Baker v. Nelson* (191 N.W. 2d 185 [1971]), the Court turned in the verdict that the Minnesota "statute governing marriage does not authorize marriage between persons of the same sex."[6] The Court cited two dictionary definitions to establish the common usage of marriage; both definitions were taken to be "based upon the fundamental difference in sex."[7] This being the case, the Court viewed the petitioners as "posing a rhetorical demand."[8] Rather than finding an irrational and invidious discrimination, this Court instead found the following expressed in the Minnesota marriage statute:

> The institution of marriage as a union of man and woman, uniquely involving the procreation and rearing of children within a family, is as old as the book of Genesis. . . . This historic institution manifestly is more deeply founded than the asserted contemporary concept of marriage and societal interests for which petitioners contend.[9]

Marriage, then, neither does not, nor cannot mean anything but what it means within the context of this tradition, going back to the first book of the Hebrew Bible. Maintaining this meaning, however, is not itself a legitimate secular purpose.

Two years after the Minnesota case, another arose, this time in Kentucky. Citing *Baker* as precedent, this Court found all the constitutional issues taken care of in that earlier case.[10] The *Jones* Court also sought help from the dictionary, checking out the definitions in three dictionaries, and found the appellants definitionally prohibited from marrying each other. The ruling stated the following: "A license to enter into a status or a relationship which the parties are incapable of achieving is a nullity. . . . In substance . . . what they propose is not a marriage."[11] The Court grounded its ruling on having been "presented with no authority to the contrary" that marriage is only opposite-sex.[12] But the Court used an implicitly religious authority to cite the fact that "[m]arriage was a custom long before the state commenced to issue licenses for that purpose," and to take note of the practice of church involvement in record-keeping.[13] It did not occur to this Court that, given the gravity of the issue—denying the right to marry—it should perhaps look further than to the dictionary, custom, and church records. In addition, the *Jones* Court cited *Reynolds* to assert the supremacy of the civil law, but made no move to accommodate the religious freedom it acknowledged was being asserted by the plaintiffs.[14] Here, an exemption for this first couple—an accommodation—made no sense because of the couple's "own incapability of entering into a marriage as that term is defined."[15] What prevented the *Jones* Court from seeing in the religious expression before it an as yet unencountered definition?

Within a year of the *Jones* decision, a case arose in the State of Washington that to all extent and purposes replayed in expanded fashion the maneuvers of the earlier case.[16] In *Singer*, the Court focused its attention on the crucial procreational and childrearing role of marriage in society in support of the argument by definition, and questioned the queer sort of family a same-sex marriage would create. In order to distinguish challenges based on *Loving* and *Perez*, the *Singer* Court found that "appellants are not being denied entry into the marriage relationship because of their sex; rather . . . because of the recognized definition of that relationship as one which may be entered into only by two persons who are members of the opposite sex."[17] The *Singer* Court's decision, then, is because of "sex," but not really. Here, the Court embraces the "societal values associated with the propagation of the human race" argument, in which the institution of marriage is embedded.[18] At bottom, it is neither "sex," nor "propagation" of the species, but "the state's recognition that our society as a whole views marriage as the appropriate and desirable forum for procreation and the rearing of children."[19] Again, the concentric circles lead to unarticulated majoritarian values that undergird the institution of marriage, values which remained unremarked in *Singer* and may be constitutionally suspect, unless propagation of the species through heteroexclusive interpersonal relationships is itself a legitimate governmental objective that validly may imply a separate caste for same-sex couples, with or without children.

The final case we will discuss cited *Singer*, but found "the most important precedent is *Baker v. Nelson*."[20] The *Adams* Court appealed to some dictionary definitions, but found it "impossible and unthinkable, and in bad faith" to accept that someone could believe he was married to someone of the same sex.[21] The finding in *Adams* was never in serious doubt, given the religious nature of the convictions which were operative before any constitutional lens entered into play, and antecedently in force. In the following passages the *Adams* Court elides processes of definition and jurisprudence; the entire line of reasoning is presented below:

> The definition of marriage, the rights and responsibilities implicit in that relationship, and the protections and preferences afforded to marriage, are now governed by the civil law. The English civil law took its attitudes and basic principles from canon law. . . . Canon law in both Judaism and Christianity could not possibly sanction any marriage between persons of the same sex because of the vehement condemnation in the scriptures of both religions. . . . Thus there has been for centuries a combination of scriptural and canonical teaching under which a "marriage" between persons of the same sex was unthinkable and, by definition, impossible. The legal protection and special status afforded to marriage . . . has historically . . . *been rationalized as being for the purpose of encouraging the propagation of the race.*[22]

Two points in the above quoted passages from *Adams* bear mentioning.

First, it seems that only the geographic jurisdiction has changed, from the dubious jurisdictions of "Judaism" and "Christianity" to that of English canon law, and then into the American regime of law. That does not, however, answer the constitutional question, especially since "vehement condemnation" is to be found in what, it is asserted, are foundational sources for making determinations in American law. It is as if had there only been another voice in the past, when the relevant thinking and definition-making was underway that has endured the test of time so well as to become definitional for us today, then automatically governing the marital relationship after a heteronormative fashion would be a different, far less automatic matter for us. The line of reasoning in *Adams* ignores the significant dangers to dissent from popular and enforced majority opinion way back when, and so serves to highlight the difference our constitutional protections make in some, but not all, cases of dissent from the prevailing standards.

Second, the move in the highlighted passages from *Adams* strongly resemble the maneuver in *McGowan* to hide the actual meaning and values protected through law under several layers of secular purpose, or, here, rationalization. One opponent of same-sex marriage performs this maneuver less artfully:

> To define a heritage is not an easy task when talking about something as broad and amorphous as the Judeo-Christian heritage. . . . While it is difficult

> to articulate a nonfaith rationale for the distinction made by the Judeo-Christian heritage between same-sex and opposite-sex marriage, the task is not impossible. . . . Unprovable assumptions have their own legitimate role to play in advancing the "compelling" interests of society.[23]

Buchanan's argument is a stretch, on his own admission; this is peculiar for something regarded to be so clearly defined as to be obvious or "linchpin." Why should the marriage rights of American citizens who happen to be gay or lesbian be held hostage for reason of a supposedly next to impossible argument, where sectarian assumptions play the major role? Just as in *McGowan*, in *Adams* we can actually perceive through the reasoning of the Court the *shadow establishment* going undercover. Surely secular rationalization can work the same "word magic" on the ban on same-sex marriage.

∽

Our point in the above analyses of Part IV has been to highlight, not the injured party and take that as a basis for analogy, but, rather, to highlight the nature of the supporting rationale for this arguably impermissible injury. This approach brings out the point: why should any nonbelievers who wish to marry be prevented from doing so ultimately for religious reasons that believers tacitly construe as universally applicable and properly expressed in the law?[24]

In conclusion, we return to the Court in *Yick Wo v. Hopkins*, from which the book's opening quotation came: "No reason for it is shown, and the conclusion cannot be resisted, that no reason for it exists except hostility to the race and nationality to which the petitioners belong, and which in the eye of the law is not justified."[25] Here, "it" is a sectarian-inspired marriage ban that impermissibly discriminates against certain persons who wish to realize their fundamental right to marry the person of their choice and share living as a couple fully entitled to all the benefits of this constitutionally-protected civil status. The vehicle of the *shadow establishment* has allowed us to understand the *de jure* ban on same-sex marriage as a naked preference for religion established in the law, an injury to many Americans the United States Constitution is designed to prevent through the no-establishment clause in its First Amendment.

Conclusion

For if the constitutional conception of "equal protection of the laws" means anything, it must at the very least mean that a bare congressional desire to harm a politically unpopular group cannot constitute a legitimate governmental interest.[1]

We have presented the case for a First Amendment-Establishment Clause understanding and invalidation of the ban against same-sex marriage. In presenting this case, the argument has connected a variety of issues and surveyed several representative lines of reasoning; a summary of the path of the argument may be helpful.

In the Introduction we noted the ban on same-sex marriage, and the features that establish the context of the secular public interest in marriage; we then posed the question: Why not allow same-sex couples to marry?

In Part I we presented marriage in the eyes of the law—a civil contract on which the legal authority confers status—where it appears a purely secular arrangement, yet we found it enmeshed in a particular normative framework, one that goes a long way to explaining recent events in state law and DOMA, which foreclose the legal recognition of same-sex marriage.

In Part II we uncovered the supporting rationale for the regulation of marriage in the law, finding it to fall under the category of morals discourse, and suggested that legislation of this perspectival sort is not based on constitutionally legitimate public policy grounds, but is instead an instance of sectarian majoritarianism, the accommodation of which is in dispute. We also presented the argument of law professor David Richards, that at issue here is an impermissible entanglement of church and state in violation of the religion clauses of the First

108 LIBERAL CONSTITUTIONALISM

Amendment. The ban on same-sex marriage is a sectarian preference that unconstitutionally restricts gay persons' conscientiously chosen identity, infringing on their freedom of religious expression. The ban, then, is arbitrary from another, equally protected, perspective under freedom of conscience. Given the polarization of this issue in communities of faith, the ban may well be considered arbitrary as well by people from within several religious traditions. It is again ironic that people from within the same religious tradition that gives the sense of rightfulness to the ban in the law, nevertheless recognize it as an arbitrary act of the civil authority.

In Part III we followed the Court in identifying the *shadow establishment*, a deeply hidden establishment in the law of majoritarian religious nonpreferentialism, disguised as legitimate public purpose, that unobjectionably accommodates freedom of religious expression, which is an establishment nonetheless and so likely unconstitutional. We also focused critical attention on the notion that same-sex marriage is an oxymoron, and so should not receive recogniton in the law.

In Part IV we let ourselves be guided by the notion of a *shadow establishment* as we browsed through the analogies to religion-based marriage discrimination in some major court cases regarding interracial and plural marriage, as well as same-sex marriage and homosexuality. Here we concluded our investigation by pulling together the many aforementioned strands into the proposition that *the ban on same-sex marriage is in effect an establishment of religion*. Given the fundamentality of the liberty interest and protected right at issue, this ban represents an in-all-likelihood impermissible expression of sectarian preference in the law, a profoundly unconstitutional and arbitrary legislative choice.

∽

The question has been answered: there is no constitutionally valid ground not to permit same-sex marriage. That is to say, to extend to same-sex couples the same legal status of marriage, with all the benefits thereunto as well as the burdens and responsibilities. We have uncovered the nature of what is being protected, what gives the ban on same-sex marriage its sense of being "good," the right policy for the nation, at least in the eyes of America's religious and political majority.

In the American context, which features marriage as a fundamental right and liberty interest, and given the public policy considerations already addressed in the law that delimit the secular purposes of marriage legislation as presented in the Introduction, only religion broadly conceived remains to explain the spirit of the laws. This, we have argued, evinces a sectarian rationale that is an invidious ground for upholding the ban on same-sex marriage against American citizens who happen to be gay or lesbian and who would like to marry their beloved in the eyes of the law. Currently, however, a sectarian perspective is established *sub silentio* in the law without benefit or real cover of legitimate secular purpose. The misperceived public interest at stake is a sham that works a world of hurt on adult individuals who would like to marry the person of their choice, as any similarly situated heterosexual person may.

The pedigree of the ban in traditional understandings and seminal court rulings on marriage law, as well as the sense of the ban on same-sex marriage, or the quality of reasonableness that many Americans find in it, we have argued, demonstrate that in the first instance the ban affects not same-sex couples, but individual American citizens who happen not to be heterosexual. As with anti-same-sex sodomy laws, the ban is tantamount to forbidding a certain love between individuals, if not those individuals themselves, were it possible legislatively so to estrange a portion of the American citizenry. The ban cannot but reflect a purely morals judgment that is inappropriately rendered into the law of the land in the liberal-democratic setting, where, in this case, no sound public policy rationale supports it.

American citizens are accustomed to understanding that the purpose of their government is to secure their rights to "life, liberty, and the pursuit of happiness," and American citizens have across the years exercised their freedom in forming marital bonds of their own choosing in the face of received custom. Hartog recounts this aspect of American history, and debunks the facile notion of there having always been one enduring form of marriage in the United States:

> Europeans and other non-Americans saw the American marital regimes, their freedoms, their possibilities for remaking identities, and they were drawn to come. This was one, usually unspoken, feature of the American ideal, of the ideal of freedom that America offered.... Like us, the men and women of the nineteenth century believed their marriages were their own individual possessions. Others might have an interest as well—children, parents, other family members, God, perhaps the state. But first of all, their marriages belonged to them. They would rarely have thought of themselves as makers of law.[2]

The marital bond between two people may represent the most interpersonal and intimate kind of happiness desired by all ordinary human beings, and ought not be infringed on by the State in the service of a sense of marriage that is sectarian in nature and tantamount to an impermissible establishment of religion in violation of the Establishment Clause.

Though many people of goodwill may also be subscribers to the traditional heteroexclusive view of marriage, they might nonetheless want to disagree with the ban on same-sex marriage because their dedication to the nation's foundational principle of equal American citizenship proves so much more compelling than does theirs to this newly revealed heterosexual, sectarian privilege. If this book has persuaded those persons to reevaluate their position, or even to change their minds, then perhaps sometime the day will dawn when those Americans who happen to be gay or lesbian will have arrived as equal citizens because their marriage relationships are legally recognized on an equal footing with their fellow citizens, and they individually are granted all the worth and dignity befitting an American citizen. To paraphrase an idea Hart used in his argument against Devlin, we should compare such a change in the law and majority opinion "not to the violent overthrow of government but to a peaceful constitutional change in its form, consistent not only with the preservation of a society but with its advance."[3]

Just as heresy called Christianity into doubt, or even into contempt, some believe that being an openly gay or lesbian person calls into doubt a hidden orthodoxy in the law reflecting the nation's religious heritage, its decreasingly *de facto* Protestant society, and so view the ban on same-sex marriage as legitimate, righteous, and "good." Lord Devlin's homosexuality-treason nexus notwithstanding, there are no heretics in this land, except those so rendered by the law merely for that purpose. And in the United States that is not only an impermissible purpose, but odious and un-American.

The American political regime was founded on liberal-democratic principles that are concerned, among other things, to protect dissenters from majoritarian opinion as may become manifest in the law to the detriment of their ability equally to enjoy their rights and liberties. The notion of the *shadow establishment* reveals that these principles are not yet as fully in place as they might be, at least not with respect to the nation's marriage laws, where some Americans continue to be burdened by the thinly veiled religious preferences of others, the impact of which is in no way benign. The notion of the *shadow establishment*, if useful, points the way to where there remains some work that must be done in order better to realize the promise of American society to all its citizens. This notion allows us to see it now, that today American citizens who happen to be gay or lesbian, among others, are threatened no less than is the constitutional order itself, by the presence of a politically powerful sectarian bias esconced in public law under sham secular rubric.

Table of Cases

Adams v. Howerton, 486 F.Supp. 1119 (1980)
Baehr v. Lewin, 852 P.2d 44 (Hawaii 1993)
Baker v. Nelson, 191 N.W. 2d 185 (1971)
Barnes v. Glen Theatre, Inc., 111 S. Ct. 2456 (1991)
Board of Education v. Barnette, 319 U.S. 624 (1943)
Bowers v. Hardwick, 478 U.S. 186 (1986)
Bradwell v. Illinois, 21 L.Ed 442 (1873)
Braunfeld Et. Al. v. Brown, 366 U.S. 599 (1961)
Brause v. Bureau of Vital Statistics, No. 3AN-95–6562 CI, 1998 WL 88743 (Alaska Super. Ct. Feb. 27, 1998)
Church of the Holy Trinity v. United States, 143 U.S. 457 (1892)
Cleveland v. United States, 329 U.S. 14 (1946)
Cleveland Bd. Of Educ. v. LaFleur, 414 U.S. 632 (1974)
Davis v. Beason, 33 L.Ed 637 (1890)
Dawson v. Vance, 329 F.Supp. 1320 (1971)
Dean v. District of Columbia, 653 A.2d 307 (D.C. 1995)
Doe v. Commonwealth, 403 F.Supp. 1199 (1975)
Everson v. Board of Education, 330 U.S. 1 (1947)
Griswold v. Connecticut, 381 U.S. 479 (1965)
In the Matter of the Adoption of . . . v. Vaughn Fischer and Sharane Fischer, 808 P.2d 1083 (Utah 1991)
Jones v. Hallahan, Ky., 501 S.W. 2d 588 (1973)
Late Corporation of Latter-day Saints and Romney v. United States, 34 L.Ed 478 (1890)
Lee v. Weisman, 122 S.Ct. 2649 (1992)
Lemon v. Kurtzman, 403 U.S. 602 (1971)
Loving v. Virginia, 388 U.S. 1 (1967)
Maynard v. Hill, 31 L.Ed. 654 (1888)

McCollum v. Board of Education, 333 U.S. 203 (1948)
McGowan v. Maryland, 366 U.S. 420 (1961)
McLaughlin v. Florida, 379 U.S. 184 (1964)
Murphy v. Ramsey, 29 L.Ed 47 (1884)
Musser v. Utah, 333 U.S. 95 (1948)
Perez v. Lippold, 198 P.2d 17 (California, 1948)
Potter v. Murray City I, 585 F.Supp. 1126 (1984)
Potter v. Murray City II, 760 F.2d 1065 (1985)
Powell v. State, 510 S.E.2d 18 (Georgia 1998)
Reynolds v. United States, 25 L.Ed 244 (1879)
Romer v. Evans, 116 S.Ct. 1620 (1996)
Salisbury v. List, 501 F. Supp. 105 (1980)
Sharma v. Sharma, 667 P.2d 395 (Kan.App. 1983)
Singer v. Hara Wash.App., 522 P.2d 1187 (1974)
Singh v. Boyes, 83 Cal. App. 2d 256 (1948)
Skinner v. Oklahoma, 316 U.S. 535 (1942)
Stan Baker, et al. v. State of Vermont, et al., 170 Vt. 194 (1999)
Torasco v. Watkins, 367 U.S. 488 (1961)
United States v. Seeger, 380 U.S. 163 (1965)
U.S. Dept. of Agriculture v. Moreno, 413 U.S. 528 (1973)
Welsh v. United States, 398 U.S. 333 (1970)
Yick Wo v. Hopkins, 30 L.Ed. 200 (1886)
Zablocki v. Redhail, 434 U.S. 374 (1978)
Zorach v. Clauson, 343 U.S. 306 (1952)

Notes

Introduction

1. Yick Wo v. Hopkins, 30 L.Ed 220, 227 (1886).
2. See Peter S. Wenz, *Abortion Rights as Religious Freedom* (Philadelphia: Temple University Press, 1992), p. 141. Wenz's approach to the issue of abortion is philosophically the closest to that of this book. He argues that the best explanation of the sense of what abortion foes stand for requires a sectarian understanding, without which they would have no reason for their political advocacy, all other anti-abortion arguments being sham.
3. These distinctions are ably presented in John Rawls' essay "The Idea of Public Reason Revisited," published in his *Collected Papers*, edited by Samuel Freeman (Cambridge: Harvard University Press, 1999), pp. 583–588. Wenz discusses the distinction between religious and secular, though without distinguishing secular from public, in his book, *Abortion Rights as Religious Freedom*, pp. 112, 188–189. The nature of religion, some prominent theologians have argued, is not rational, and that is how we approach it here: it can never provide a legitimate state purpose on its own terms. See the classic work, Rudolf Otto, *The Idea of the Holy: An Inquiry into the non-rational factor in the idea of the divine and its relation to the rational*, John W. Harvey, tr. (London: Oxford University Press, 1958, orig. 1923).
4. See Daniel L. Dreisbach, "The Constitution's Forgotten Religious Clause: Reflections on the Article VI Religious Test Ban," *Journal of Church and State* 38, no. 2 (Spring 1996): 261–262, 293–294.
5. In Chapter Eight we draw an important distinction between same-sex marriage and "gay marriage."
6. These benefits are numerous and vary across the States; they represent public policy aspirations and investment. Fifteen major legal rights and benefits are given in William N. Eskridge, Jr., *The Case for Same-Sex Marriage: From Sexual Liberty to Civilized Commitment* (New York: Free Press, 1996), pp. 66–67. In the recent challenge to a state's ban on same-sex marriage, the Supreme Court of Hawaii listed 14 marital rights and benefits of material interest to same-sex couples, theirs "but for the fact that they are denied access to the state-conferred legal status of marriage." See Baehr v. Lewin, 852 P.2d 44, 59 (Hawaii 1993). One law review article listed 45 rights and benefits married

couples are entitled to just in Hawaii. See Christopher J. Keller, "Divining the Priest: A Case Comment on *Baehr v. Lewin*," *Law & Inequality* 12, no. 2 (June 1994): 493–494, n.61. In the State of Vermont "a legally recognized spouse is entitled to more than three hundred state benefits and one thousand federal benefits." See Keith E. Sealing, "Article: Polygamists Out of the Closet: Statutory and State Constitutional Prohibitions Against Polygamy Are Unconstitutional Under the Free Exercise Clause," *Georgia State University Law Review* 17 (Spring 2001): 750. The issue of the exclusivity of state-conferred tax code benefits for heterosexual spouses was already noted about thirty years ago in Arthur J. Silverstein's "Comment. Constitutional Aspects of the Homosexual's Right to a Marriage License," *Journal of Family Law* 12 (1972–73): 622–623, n.60.
7. Legal arguments for gay marriage have been made for nearly three decades. For example, see Note, "The Legality of Homosexual Marriage," *Yale Law Journal* 82, no. 3 (January 1973): 573–589.
8. The following two sources are accessible to contemporary readers on the topic of same-sex marriage: Robert M. Baird and Stuart E. Rosenbaum, eds., *Same-Sex Marriage: The Moral and Legal Debate* (Amherst: Prometheus, 1997), and, Andrew Sullivan, ed., *Same-Sex Marriage: Pro and Con. A Reader* (New York: Vintage Books/Random House, 1997). These readers contain source material and commentary across a wide range of related issues, far beyond the narrow scope of this work.
9. For a contemporary perspective, see E. J. Graff, *What Is Marriage For?: The Strange Social History of Our Most Intimate Institution* (Boston: Beacon Press, 1999). For an historical perspective, see Jack Goody, *The Development of the Family and Marriage in Europe* (Cambridge: Cambridge University Press, 1983), which arrays "Eastern" and "Western" Mediterranean differences in ways of describing family life, social structures, and marriage, and traces the emergence of ecclesiastical control over marriage and the family.
10. The question of "purpose" in connection with marriage, procreation, and sexuality, is pursued in Igor Primoratz, *Ethics and Sex* (London: Routledge, 1999), pp. 16–17, which argues that the notion of "purpose" implies someone whose purpose it is, as in human sexual choices subscribing or not to "God's purpose."
11. The essay is David A. J. Richards, "Sexual Preference as a Suspect (Religious) Classification: An Alternative Perspective on the Unconstitutionality of Anti-Lesbian/Gay Initiatives," *Ohio State Law Journal* 55, no. 3 (1994): 491–553.
12. Though this may characterize public policy generally, the "factual" basis of the ban on same-sex marriage might need more demythologizing, than reasoned rebuttal. See Pamela S. Katz, "The Case for Legal Recognition of Same-Sex Marriage," *Journal of Law & Policy* 8 (1999): 64–73.
13. Information regarding the state of sodomy law in the United States was taken on July 13, 2001, from the web site of Lambda Legal Defense and Education Fund (LLDEF), the premier gay rights legal advocacy organization in the United States, at >>www.lambdalegal.org/cgi-bin/pages/states/sodomy<<. The first State to repeal its sodomy law was Illinois in 1962, though the American Law Institute Model Penal Code recommended its deletion in 1955.
14. For the best treatment of the widespread effects of sodomy laws, whether enforced or not, across all fifty states, see Christopher R. Leslie, "Creating Crimi-

nals: The Injuries Inflicted by "Unenforced" Sodomy Laws," *Harvard Civil Rights–Civil Liberties Law Review* 35(Winter 2000). Leslie usefully discusses how sodomy laws are "enforced by mechanisms short of criminal prosecution, conviction, and imprisonment," indirectly, through various forms of state-sponsored discrimination. See Ibid., 136.
15. On July 13, 2001, LLDEF reports that in June of 2000 a Texas court overturned that state's sodomy law. See >>www.lambdalegal.org/cgi-bin/pages/documents/record?record=275<<.
16. The statute as given above remained in effect in the 1990 Revision of the Code of Georgia Annotated, though it has since been invalidated (*Powell v. State*, 510 S.E.2d 18 [1998]).
17. For example, Harvard University Law Professor Laurence H. Tribe, who argued the case in *Bowers* on behalf of Michael Hardwick against Georgia's sodomy statute, reflects on the experience in his essay "Contrasting Constitutional Visions: Of Real and Unreal Differences," *Harvard Civil Rights-Civil Liberties Law Review* 22, no. 1(Winter 1987): 95–109. Also see the discussion of *Bowers* in Richard A. Posner, *Sex and Reason* (Cambridge: Harvard University Press, 1992). Posner finds antisodomy statutes to have "a quality of invidiousness. . . . a gratuitousness, an egregiousness, a cruelty, and a meanness." See Ibid., p. 346.
18. Leslie, "Creating Criminals," 171–172.
19. Ibid., 110.
20. See the LLDEF web site at >>www.lambdalegal.org/cgi-bin/pages/documents/record?record=217<<, visited on July 13, 2001. In addition to those States and DC, many cities and counties have gay rights civil ordinances, policies, or proclamations. The reader should check the specific statute for further information as to what exactly it covers.
21. That this is not the case is roundly treated by Kenneth Sherrill in his *Affidavit* in the case of *Joseph C. Steffan v. Richard Cheney, Secretary of Defense*, entitled "On Gay People as a Politically Powerless Group," published in Marc Wolinsky and Kenneth Sherrill, eds., *Gays and the Military: Joseph Steffan versus the United States* (Princeton: Princeton University Press, 1993), pp. 84–120.
22. A transcript of the oral argument, published by Alderson Reporting Company, Inc., was obtained from Lambda Legal Defense and Education Fund, Inc., of New York. David A. J. Richards, in Chapter Seven of his recent book, *Women, Gays, and the Constitution: The Grounds for Feminism and Gay Rights in Culture and Law* (Chicago: University of Chicago Press, 1998), takes issue with Justice Scalia's dissenting opinion in *Romer*, which argued that gay rights ordinances establish "special rights" contrary to a legitimate governmental purpose, the legislation of majoritarian morality *simpliciter*.
23. For example, see Charlotte J. Patterson, "Children of Lesbian and Gay Parents," *Child Development* 63, no. 5 (October 1992): 1025–1042. Patterson's essay is a review of the expanding literature in this area, which concludes unequivocally that "[e]xisting research evidence provides no justification for denial of parental rights and responsibilities to lesbians and gay men on the basis of their sexual orientation." See Ibid., 1037.
24. For example, see Gregory M. Herek's law review essay, "Myths About Sexual Orientation: A Lawyer's Guide to Social Science Research," *Law & Sexuality* 1

118 LIBERAL CONSTITUTIONALISM

(1991): 133–172, which reviews several inaccurate characterizations of persons who are not heterosexual.
25. For example, see Robert L. Barret and Bryan E. Robinson, "Gay Dads," in Adele Eskeles Gottfried and Allen W. Gottfried, eds., *Redefining Families: Implications for Children's Development* (New York: Plenum Press, 1994), pp. 157–170.
26. Numerical information taken from Leslie, "Creating Criminals," 147. Information regarding the rapidly changing state of adoption law in the United States was taken on July 31, 2001, from the LLDEF web-site, at >>www.lambdalegal.org/cgi-bin/pages/documents/record?record=399<<. The reader is cautioned to note that even where second-parent adoption by gay persons is permitted or common practice, the level of resistance to any such adoption during a hearing may range from little to high in any individual case, and is dependent on such factors as the proclivity of the local judge.
27. One early review of the literature on gay and lesbian parents in child custody cases found a consistent failure to document any evidence substantiating fears of the inferiority of homosexual-oriented parents. See David J. Kleber, et al., "The Impact of Parental Homosexuality in Child Custody Cases: A Review of the Literature," originally published in 1986, reprinted in Wayne K. Dynes and Stephen Donaldson, eds., *Homosexuality: Discrimination, Criminology, and the Law,* Garland Studies in Homosexuality Volume VI (New York: Garland, 1992), pp. 323–329. Also see G. Dorsey Green and Frederick W. Bozett, "Lesbian Mothers and Gay Fathers," in John C. Gonsiorek and James D. Weinrich, eds., *Homosexuality: Research Implications for Public Policy* (Newbury Park: SAGE, 1991), pp. 197–214; and Patricia J. Falk, "The Gap between Psychosocial Assumptions and Empirical Research in Lesbian-Mother Custody Cases," in Gottfried and Gottfried, eds., *Redefining Families,* pp. 131–156.
28. For example, see Claudia A. Lewis, "From This Day Forward: A Feminine Moral Discourse on Homosexual Marriage," *Yale Law Journal* 97, no. 8 (July 1988): 1791, which presents the following argument:

> Reality belies the myth of homosexuals as aberrant loners who bear no relation to the tenderness associated with marriage and the family. Only a pathological twist of the social memory forgets that homosexuals are born into and raised by families. . . . Like heterosexuals, homosexuals desire the warmth and security of intimate relationships created by marriage and the family. The human proclivity for forming traditional family bonds is deeply socially ingrained and not dependent on sexual orientation.

29. See Jan E. Dizard and Howard Gadlin, *The Minimal Family* (Amherst: University of Massachusetts Press, 1990), pp. 9, 23.
30. See the LLDEF web site at >>www.lambdalegal.org/cgi-bin/pages/documents/record?record=403<<, visited on July 13, 2001. Gay persons as couples seem to function similiarly to other couples. See Lawrence A. Kurdek and J. Patrick Smith, "Relationship Quality of Partners in Heterosexual Married, Heterosexual Cohabiting, and Gay and Lesbian Relationships," *Journal of Personality and Social Psychology* 51, no. 4 (October 1986): 711–720. Some popular stereotypes about gay persons' intimate partnerships are debunked in Letitia Anne Peplau, "Lesbian and Gay Relationships," in Gonsiorek and Weinrich, eds., *Homosexuality: Research Implications for Public Policy,* pp. 179–186.

31. Interestingly, although the United States House of Representatives provides for a domestic partner registry, the House has barred the District of Columbia from implementing one of its own.
32. See the LLDEF web site at >>www.lambdalegal.org/cgi-bin/pages/documents/record?record=21<<, visited on July 13, 2001.
33. Census 2000 results on households is given in Census Brief 2000, "Housing Characteristics: 2000," issued October, 2001, and published by the Department of Commerce, Economics and Statistics Administration.
34. See Edwin M. Schur, *Labeling Women Deviant: Gender, Stigma, and Social Control* (New York: Random House, 1984), pp. 52–54. The Hawaii Legislature's marriage statute restricting the marital relationship to a male and a female was held on its face to discriminate on the basis of sex because it did not allow women to do what it allowed men to do (i.e., marry a woman), and vice-versa. This court, however, did not extend the boundaries of the fundamental right of marriage in Hawaii to include same-sex couples. One interesting discussion of *Baehr* as locating sexual orientation discrimination under gender discrimination is Jordan Herman, "The Fusion of Gay Rights and Feminism: Gender Identity and Marriage After *Baehr v. Lewin*," *Ohio State Law Journal* 56, no. 3 (1995): 985–1018.
35. For example, see J. Michael Bailey, "Gender Identity," in Ritch C. Savin-Williams and Kenneth M. Cohen, eds., *The Lives of Lesbians, Gays, and Bisexuals: Children to Adults* (Fort Worth: Harcourt Brace & Company, 1996). This volume's other chapters also present information and analyses based in policy-relevant social science research.
36. See Baehr v. Lewin, 852 P.2d 44 (Hawaii 1993).
37. Other features of local or state public policy might include a hate crimes ordinance which includes sexual orientation. In addition and increasingly, major corporations and unions have extended the same package of benefits to their gay or lesbian employees' life partners as they already do to their other employees' life partners. LLDEF estimates that approximately 23% of firms employing 5,000 or more workers provides health benefits to nontraditional partners, a percentage that is increasing by the week. See the LLDEF web site at >>www.lambdalegal.org/cgi-bin/pages/documents/record?record=18<<, visited on July 13, 2001.
38. Law Professor Cass R. Sunstein discusses the rational basis test, also known as rationality review or the irrationality argument, in connection with equality and the issue of same-sex marriage, and identifies the Equal Protection Clause of the Fourteenth Amendment as an anti-caste principle in "Homosexuality and the Constitution," *Indiana Law Journal* 70 (Winter 1994): 1–28.

Part I. Marriage in the Law

1. Maynard v. Hill, 31 L.Ed. 654, 657, 659–660 (1888) (citations omitted).
2. During the nineteenth century, for example, when common-law marriages were prevalent, there was a considerable variation in understanding concerning the marriage relationship and what constitutes a marriage, which left ample room for judicial discretion and personal predilection. See Stuart J.

Stein, "Common-Law Marriage: Its History and Certain Contemporary Problems," *Journal of Family Law* 9 (1970): 271–299. Space does not permit us to investigate the historical emergence of secular control over marriage regulation and the decline of ecclesiastical authority, or the relationship of either to the interesting endurance of the common law. See the discussion in Geoffrey May, *Marriage Laws and Decisions in the United States. A Manual* (New York: Russell Sage Foundation, 1929), pp. 5–12. Historical documents of religious and secular legislation on the family and marriage are usefully gathered in Sophonisba Breckenridge, *The Family and the State. Select Documents* (Chicago: University of Chicago Press, 1934). Useful excavations of early American history as regards gay persons, marriage, and the law can be found in Dwight J. Penas, "Bless The Tie That Binds: A Puritan-Covenant Case for Same-Sex Marriage," *Law & Inequality* 8, no. 3 (July 1990): 533–565; and, Anne B. Goldstein, "History, Homosexuality, and Political Values: Searching for the Hidden Determinants of *Bowers v. Hardwick*," *Yale Law Journal* 97, no. 6 (May 1988): 1073–1103.

Chapter One. Marriage as Contract and Status

1. See Kenneth L. Karst's pathbreaking law review essay, "The Freedom of Intimate Association," *Yale Law Journal* 89, no. 4 (March 1980): 667, 671.
2. A useful presentation and discussion of the emergence of the recognition of marriage as a fundamental right is presented and discussed in Henry H. Foster, Jr., "Marriage: A Basic Civil Right of Man," *Fordham Law Review* 37 (1968–69): 51–80.
3. 316 U.S. 535, 538, 541 (1942).
4. 414 U.S. 632, 639–640 (1974).
5. Salisbury v. List, 501 F.Supp. 105 (1980).
6. Section 451.010, Chapter 451, Marriage, Marriage Contracts, and Rights of Married Women, under Title XXX, Domestic Relations, Annotated Missouri Statutes, 1978.
7. Paragraph 10, under Article 3, New York Domestic Relations Law, 1992.
8. Paragraph 420(b) under Division 3, Marriage, 1992 California Family Code.
9. Paragraph 457:31, Chapter 457, Marriages, under Title XLIII, Domestic Relations, New Hampshire Revised Statutes Annotated, 1983.
10. Paragraph 2–406 under Title 2, Family Law, Annotated Code of the General Laws of Maryland, 1984. A state's particular religious heritage is reflected in the following statute from South Carolina: "Only ministers of the Gospel or accepted Jewish rabbis and officers authorized to administer oaths in this State are authorized to administer a marriage ceremony in this State." (Paragraph 20-1-20 under Title 20, Domestic Relations, Code of Laws of South Carolina Annotated, 1976).
11. Paragraph 25-1-1 under Title 25, Domestic Relations, South Dakota Codified Laws, 1984 Revision.
12. Sections 19-3-4 and 19-3-7 of Chapter 3, Marriage Generally, of the 1990 Revision of the Annotated Code of Georgia.

13. For example, see Lawrence Stone, *Uncertain Unions: Marriage in England 1660–1753* (Oxford: Oxford University Press, 1992).
14. See David Boaz, *Libertarianism: A Primer* (New York: Free Press, 1997), pp. 241–242.
15. See the analysis of *Zablocki* in Laurence C. Nolan, "The Meaning of Loving: Marriage, Due Process and Equal Protection (1967–1990) as Equality and Marriage, from Loving to Zablocki," *Howard Law Journal* 41 (Winter 1998): 247, 267.
16. "Status is personal and therefore travels with the individual: status is 'performed' wherever a person goes." See Note, "In Sickness and in Health, in Hawaii and Where Else?: Conflict of Laws and Recognition of Same-Sex Marriages," *Harvard Law Review* 109, no. 8 (June 1996): 2039, n.8. By suggesting that marriage is performative, we evoke Judith Butler's idea of gender (another status) as performative and so amenable to limitless individual variation whatever the regulative categories imposed on the institution of marriage might happen to be. The regulative category at issue here is heterosexuality as a normative regime. See Judith Butler, *Gender Trouble: Feminism and the Subversion of Identity* (New York: Routledge, 1990).
17. Plural marriages (e.g., polygamy) are discussed in Chapter Seven.
18. The issue of gay persons and the form *vs.* substance of marriage is discussed in Chapter Eight.
19. See Milton C. Regan, Jr., *Family Law and the Pursuit of Intimacy* (New York: New York University Press, 1993), p. 118.
20. See Harry D. Krause, *Family Law. In A Nutshell*, Third Edition (St. Paul: West Publishing Co., 1995), pp. 3, 40.
21. See Regan, *Family Law and the Pursuit of Intimacy*, p. 120.
22. See Ibid., p. 122.
23. See David L. Chambers, "What If? The Legal Consequences of Marriage and the Legal Needs of Lesbian and Gay Male Couples," *Michigan Law Review* 95, no. 2 (November 1996): 447. Chambers is critical of accepting the protections, legal consequences, and other considerations of a domestic partner registration law, given that these laws are usually less generous in the benefits that they do bestow than are laws regarding married spouses. See Ibid., 488.
24. A slightly different view is offered by Sally Goldfarb in her law review essay, "Family Law, Marriage, and Heterosexuality: Questioning the Assumptions," *Temple Political & Civil Rights Law Review* 7 (Spring 1998). Goldfarb argues that it is the physical aspects themselves of heterosexual intimacy that anchor the ban on same-sex marriage, heterosexual intercourse itself being the essence of marriage, without any morals edifice beneath or above. This essay may miss the sense of what is being protected, as in DOMA. Another law review essay links the in-house procreation requirement to an abridgement of the expressive purpose of marriage. See David B. Cruz, "'Just Don't Call It Marriage': The First Amendment and Marriage as an Expressive Resource," *Southern California Law Review* 74 (May 2001). Cruz believes that insistence on the "mixed-sex dyad" expresses a value that can only be understood as moral or sectarian. See Ibid., 1004–1007.
25. See Jo VanEvery, "Heterosexuality and domestic life," in Diane Richardson, ed., *Theorising Heterosexuality: Telling it Straight* (Buckingham: Open University Press, 1996), pp. 40, 52.

26. The general lack of disestablishment in family law is discussed in Carol Weisbrod, "Family, Church, and State: An Essay on Constitutionalism and Religious Authority," in Diana Tietjens Meyers, et al., eds., *Kindred Matters: Rethinking the Philosophy of the Family* (Ithaca: Cornell University Press, 1993), pp. 228–256.
27. A noteworthy exception is Jonathan Ned Katz, *the Invention of HeteroSEXUALITY* (New York: Dutton/Penguin, 1995), which argues that heterosexuality is "always already there," a "silent certainty," a "hidden persuader."
28. See James B. Nelson, "Where Are We? Seven Sinful Problems and Seven Virtuous Possibilities," Chapter Sixteen in Kieran Scott and Michael Warren, eds., *Perspectives on Marriage: A Reader,* Second Edition (New York: Oxford University Press, 2001), pp. 180, 181.
29. For example, see the now classic work by Daniel A. Helminiak, *What the Bible Really Says About Homosexuality,* Millennium Edition (Tajique, NM: Alamo Square Press, 2000).
30. For example, Law Professor George W. Dent, Jr., devotes a section of his law review essay to the argument that same-sex marriage ought to be legally proscribed because it is apt to fuel hostility to religion, in "The Defense of Traditional Marriage," *Journal of Law & Politics* 15 (Fall 1999): 640–641.
31. Regarding this inscription, "the judiciary has unanimously inferred prohibitions of same-sex marriage from silent state statutes" and has "relied on the premise that a lawful marriage, by definition, can be entered into only by two persons of the opposite sex." See Irving J. Sloan, *Homosexual Conduct and the Law* (New York: Oceana, 1987), p. 33. We address the view of same-sex marriage being an oxymoron, given "marriage, by definition," in Chapter Six.

Chapter Two. The Defense of Marriage Act and Recent Events in State Law

1. Prominent theologian Reinhold Niebuhr, quoted in Dennis Altman, Global Sex (Chicago: University of Chicago Press, 2001), p. 138.
2. See Kathleen M. Sands, "Public, Pubic, and Private: Religion in Political Discourse," Chapter Three in her edited volume, *God Forbid: Religion and Sex in American Public Life* (New York: Oxford University Press, 2000). Sands uncovers a hidden religious preference in legal reactions to sexual dissidence, and presents sexuality as protected under freedom of conscience, just like religious differences, though unlike racial differences. See Ibid., pp. 70, 71.
3. See Bernard Cooke, "What God Has Joined Together . . . ," Chapter Twenty-nine in Scott and Warren, eds., *Perspectives on Marriage,* pp. 348, 351 (emphasis original).
4. See the discussion in Janet R. Jakobsen, "Why Sexual Regulation? Family Values and Social Movements," Chapter Five in Sands, ed., *God Forbid,* esp. pp. 115–119.
5. In Chapter Eight we draw and analyze the distinction between same-sex marriage and "gay marriage," and show certain of the latter to encompass heterosexual marriages in form and legality.

6. Note that this was the issue in *Loving* (388 U.S. 1[1966]), one state's refusing to recognize a duly performed marriage from another state for reason of a morals purpose expressed in its law. See Peter Wallenstein, "Law and the Boundaries of Place and Race in Interracial Marriage," *Akron Law Review* 32 (1999).
7. Baehr v. Lewin, 852 P.2d 44 (Hawaii 1993).
8. An accessible history of this series of events is given in John Gallagher, "Marriage, Hawaiian Style," *The Advocate*, Issue 726 (February 4, 1997): 22–28. An edited version of the "Report of the Hawaii Commission on Sexual Orientation and the Law" is given in Baird and Rosenbaum, eds., *Same-Sex Marriage*, pp. 211–226. This report was the state legislature's response to the decision in *Baehr*; it is a defense of traditional, opposite-sex marriage based in public policy considerations such as concern for the welfare of children and for negative effects on Hawaii's major industry, tourism, should allowance for same-sex marriage stand in the law.
9. 852 P.2d 44, 63 (Hawaii 1993). The *Loving* case is discussed in Chapter Seven.
10. No. 3AN-95-6562 CI, 1998 WL 88743 (Alaska Super. Ct. Feb. 27, 1998). The discussion of the factual events in Alaska are taken largely from Kevin G. Clarkson, David Orgon Coolidge, and William C. Duncan, "The Alaska Marriage Amendment: The People's Choice on the Last Frontier," *Alaska Law Review* 16 (December 1999).
11. This final form of the Alaska Defense of Marriage Act was passed by Alaska voters, and is given in Clarkson, et al., "The Alaska Marriage Amendment," 240.
12. 170 Vt. 194, 197 (1999) (emphasis added).
13. *Ibid.* at 208, 209.
14. 170 Vt. 194, 223 (1999).
15. *Ibid.* at 216–220 (1999).
16. A chronology and analysis of the events in Vermont, with the implications for DOMA drawn, is provided in Randall Blandin, "Baker v. Vermont: The Vermont State Supreme Court Held that Denying Same-Sex Couples the Benefits and Privileges of Marriage Is Unconstitutional," *Law & Sexuality* 9 (1999/2000). The wisdom of Vermont's new policy that denies a marriage license to same-sex couples, and instead offers them a "civil union," is analyzed in "Vermont Creates System of Civil Unions" under the "Recent Legislation" section of *Harvard Law Review* 114 (February 2001): 1421–1426.
17. See Scott Ruskay-Kidd, "The Defense of Marriage Act and the Overextension of Congressional Authority," *Columbia Law Review* 97, no. 5 (June 1997): 1451, mentioning two previous examples of where Congress has acted on its capacity to attenuate the full faith and credit clause, though never to prohibit states from extending the customary recognition, a power Congress may not in any case possess. In 1902 some members of Congress attempted to amend the United States Constitution to ban polygamy, but it met with President Theodore Roosevelt's opposition and did not make it through Congress. See Sealing, "Polygamists Out of the Closet," 704. Sealing draws a parallel between, on the one hand, the numerous anti-polygamy measures passed in the States and also at the federal level, and the attempt to amend the Constitution, and, on the other hand, the numerous contemporary measures passed in the States to clarify their marriage statutes so as to prohibit the legal recognition of same-sex marriages,

124   LIBERAL CONSTITUTIONALISM

and the drive to enact similar legislation at the national level: "It is at least curious that Congress felt that a federal constitutional amendment was needed in light of the recent Court decisions upholding draconian anti-polygamy statutes and state constitutional prohibitions against polygamy." See Ibid., 704, n.87. The implication being that then, as now, the proposed or now actual national legislation addresses no clear need or lack of law at a lower level.

18. From the enrolled bill of January 3, 1996, titled The Defense of Marriage Act / Public Law 104–199, Sections 2 and 3. This was signed into law by President Clinton on September 21, 1996.
19. The perspective of DOMA supporters that it is a pro-states' rights bill is rebutted as, at best, "heavily ironic," because it may in actuality weaken states' rights, in Ruskay-Kidd, "The Defense of Marriage Act," 1464–1465.
20. See Cass Sunstein, "Don't Panic," an excerpted selection from his expert testimony, printed in Sullivan, ed., *Same-Sex Marriage: Pro and Con*, pp. 211, 212.
21. The issue of interracial marriages is treated in Chapter Seven.
22. Representative Barr's comments from the House floor were taken on June 19, 2001, from his web site page at <www.gop.gov/oo/item-news.asp?N=20010228163906>. This Congressman was a sponsor of DOMA in the House.
23. See Chapter One in Sullivan, ed., *Same-Sex Marriage: Pro and Con*, for ten historical briefs questioning the assumption that same-sex marriage is unheard-of in the Western world.
24. Senator Coats' comments on May 9, 1996, are given on p. S4947 of the *Congressional Record*.
25. Senator Helms' comments on September 9, 1996, are given on p. S10067 of the *Congressional Record*.
26. This discussion is based in the Senate's "Senate's Record Vote Analysis" and "Synopsis" of DOMA, issued after its passage on September 10, 1996, and was taken on June 19, 2001, from the Senate's web site at <<www.senate.gov/-rpc/rva/1042/1042280.htm<<.
27. Legal scholar William N. Eskridge, Jr., argues that those fundamentalist Christian supporters of traditional majoritarian values are engaged in "a kind of identity politics" based in opposition to gay rights, as though this political position reflects what is central to their faith. See his law review essay, "No Promo Homo: The Sedimentation of Antigay Discourse and the Channeling Effect of Judicial Review," *New York University Law Review* 75 (November 2000): 1337.
28. Other advanced Western societies have chosen another course, extending legal recognition of same-sex relationships, if not of a same-sex marriage as in The Netherlands, and perhaps also now in Belgium. See Nicholas J. Patterson, "The Repercussions in the European Union of the Netherlands' Same-Sex Marriage Law," *Chicago Journal of International* Law 2 (Spring 2001), which reveals how the distinction between heterosexual and homosexual marriages has been removed, with liberalizing effects in other European Union states expected; and, Edward Brumby, "NOTE: What Is in a Name: Why the European Same-sex Partnership Acts Create a Valid Marital Relationship," *Georgia Journal of International and Comparative Law* 28 (Fall 1999), which provides a chronology with analysis of the movement in Europe to extend legal recognition and benefits to same-sex couples.

29. See Steven K. Green, "Justice David Josiah Brewer and the 'Christian Nation' Maxim," *Albany Law Review* 63 (1999). The case in which Justice Brewer uttered the maxim was *Church of the Holy Trinity v. United States*, 143 U.S. 457 (1892). Green argues that Brewer was unclear about "what it meant to call America "Christian,". . . . The phrase was not self-defining—America could be "Christian" in several senses of the word . . ." See Ibid., 447.
30. See Dent, "The Defense of Traditional Marriage," pp. 614, 618, 619, 621. This essay is usefully consulted for its lack of circumspection in presenting the case for traditional marriage and against same-sex marriage.
31. The alternative marital regimes presented in their day by interracial and plural marriages are discussed in Chapter Seven.
32. Law Professor Didi Herman offers a similar assessment for the situation of gay rights in Canada in her book, *Rights of Passage: Struggles for Lesbian & Gay Equality* (Toronto: University of Toronto Press, 1994). Her argument is that conservative, evangelical Protestants and others perceive gay rights to "epitomize the trend" towards the "increasing secularization of Canadian society"; it "is one of the most significant threats to the reaffirmation of Canada as a Christian nation." See Ibid., p. 77. Herman provides a useful discussion of the stealth tactics adopted by religious conservatives who seek to advance their sectarian cause politically, but under cover of legitimate secular purpose, in a section entitled "Legal Translation" in Ibid., pp. 109–119.
33. See Gregory Layman, *The Great Divide: Religious and Cultural Conflict in American Party Politics* (New York: Columbia University Press, 2001).
34. Ibid., pp. 260, 307.
35. See Rogers M. Smith, "'Equal' Treatment? A Liberal Separationist View," in Stephen V. Monsma and J. Christopher Soper, eds., *Equal Treatment of Religion in a Pluralistic Society* (Grand Rapids: William B. Eerdmans, 1998), pp. 181, 182.
36. Ibid., p. 197. The issue of the status of gay persons in the law and in public policy is explored at length in Gordon A. Babst, *Just Because You're Accepted Doesn't Mean You Belong: An Inquiry Into the Social Meaning and Value of American Citizenship*, unpublished dissertation, 1996.

Part II. The Law and Morality Distinction, Violated

1. *Board of Education v. Barnette*, 319 U.S. 624, 658, 653, 654 (1943) (Frankfurter, J., dissenting).
2. An accessible reader in the area of law and morality is Robert M. Baird and Stuart E. Rosenbaum, eds., *Morality and the Law* (Buffalo: Prometheus, 1988).
3. See her essay "Lesbian and Gay Rights: Pro," in Michael Leahy and Dan Cohn-Sherbok, eds., *The Liberation Debate: Rights at Issue* (London: Routledge, 1996), p. 107.
4. See Kenneth L. Karst, *Belonging to America: Equal Citizenship and the Constitution* (New Haven: Yale University Press, 1989), p. 3. Karst contrasts the principle of equal citizenship with the decision in *Bowers* in Ibid., pp. 201–210.
5. The term "heteronormativity" is discussed in Michael Warner's "Introduction" to his edited volume, *Fear of a Queer Planet: Queer Politics and Social*

126   LIBERAL CONSTITUTIONALISM

Theory (Minneapolis: University of Minnesota Press, 1993); the term may be original with him.
6. Catholic theologian Richard Peddicord offers a well-rounded religious ethics case for gay and lesbian rights. See his book, *Gay and Lesbian Rights. A Question: Sexual Ethics or Social Justice?* (Kansas City: Sheed & Ward, 1996).
7. The project of finding a better norm by exposing, critiquing, and debunking heteronormativity can be regarded as ethics work. See Patricia Beattie Jung and Ralph F. Smith, *Heterosexism: An Ethical Challenge* (Albany: State University of New York Press, 1993).

Chapter Three. Morals Discourse and Law

1. See Mark D. Jordan, *The Invention of Sodomy in Christian Theology* (Chicago: University of Chicago Press, 1997). Also see Jordan's more recent work, *The Silence of Sodom: Homosexuality in Modern Catholicism* (Chicago: University of Chicago Press, 2000), where he presents and holds to critical scrutiny some of the Catholic Church's historical and contemporary motives regarding homosexual activity.
2. Leslie describes gay persons as under a "criminal moniker," regardless of whether they actually engage in the proscribed sexual activity, or whether non-homosexual persons do. See Leslie, "Creating Criminals," 6, 7, 30.
3. See Blackstone's *Commentaries on the Laws of England: Of Public Wrongs* (Chicago: Callaghan and Company, 1884, Third Edition-Revised, 1962 [orig. 1769]), Volume 2, Book IV, Chapter 15.
4. See Ibid. (emphasis original). The modern *locus classicus* response to this approach is Louis Henkin, "Morals and the Constitution: The Sin of Obscenity," *Columbia Law Review* 63, no.3 (March, 1963): 391–414, who argues that the real motive behind morality legislation resides in religious antecedents, not in the realm of reason.
5. 478 U.S. 186, 196–197 (1986) (Burger, C.J., concurring).
6. See Robert Douglas Chesler, "Imagery of Community, Ideology of Authority: The Moral Reasoning of Chief Justice Burger," *Harvard Civil Rights-Civil Liberties Law Review* 18, no. 2 (Summer 1983): 453–482. Chesler presents Burger as "legitimizing the majority's moral hegemony and authority with the nostalgic yearning for a simpler, less 'anomic' world." See Ibid., 477.
7. See Harold P. Schombert, "*Baehr v. Lewin:* How Far Has the Door Been Opened? Finding a State Policy for Recognizing Same-Sex Marriages," *Women's Rights Law Reporter* 16, no. 3 (Spring 1995): 338.
8. Law Professor Goldstein argues that the majority and dissenting opinions in *Bowers* parallel and also recast the Devlin-Hart debate. See Goldstein, "History, Homosexuality, and Political Values," 1093–1098.
9. See *The Wolfenden Report. Report of the Committee on Homosexual Offenses and Prostitution,* Authorized American Edition (New York: Stein and Day, 1963), p. 24.
10. See Ibid., p. 48. For further elaboration on some of the points raised in the second quotation from *The Wolfenden Report,* see A. R. Louch's frequently cited essay, "Sins and Crimes," *Philosophy* 43, no. 163 (January 1968): 38–50, which

distinguishes a particular form of society and its brand of morality from morality as such, and identifies the need for clarity in the law as regards what counts as harmful injury. Also see Carl F. Cranor, "Legal Moralism Reconsidered," *Ethics* 89, no. 2 (January 1979): 147–164, which questions the alleged "comparable degrees of seriousness" between traditional victimless immoralities and violent criminal acts.

11. See Patrick Devlin's essay "The Enforcement of Morals," reprinted in Baird and Rosenbaum, eds., *Morality and the Law*, pp. 25, 26, 27, 28.
12. The distinction between socially harmful conduct and immoral conduct is given a cogent articulation in Joel Feinberg's essay "Hard Cases for the Harm Principle," reprinted in his *Social Philosophy* (Englewood Cliffs: Prentice-Hall, 1973), pp. 36–54.
13. See H. L. A. Hart, "Immorality and Treason," reprinted in Baird and Rosenbaum, eds., *Morality and the Law*, p. 47.
14. Ibid., p. 52. There are practical considerations as well when translating morals discourse into the criminal law. See Louis B. Schwartz, "Morals Offenses and the Model Penal Code," *Columbia Law Review* 63, no. 4 (April 1963): 669–686, arguing that a law for "sin control" is inherently a "constitutional infirmity"; and, Sanford H. Kadish, "The Crisis of Overcriminalization," *Annals of the American Academy of Political and Social Science* 374 (November 1967): 157–170, arguing that enforcing morals offences reduces law's claim to legitimacy.
15. See Ronald Dworkin, "Lord Devlin and the Enforcement of Morals," *Yale Law Journal* 75, no. 6 (May 1966): 986–1005.
16. See Devlin, "The Enforcement of Morals," p. 20.
17. A useful analysis of Devlin's position vis-à-vis the context of American constitutional protections is David A. J. Richards, "Sexual Autonomy and the Constitutional Right to Privacy: A Case Study in Human Rights and the Unwritten Constitution," *Hastings Law Journal* 30, no. 4 (March 1979): 957–1018, esp. 990–999.
18. Some constitutional scholars and historians will disagree here. For example, Law Professor Michael J. Perry writes that the Constitution is not a legal document, but a moral one, and so the American people have a "basic and irreducible" moral self-understanding as a religious people. What's more, we Americans "have understood [ourselves] to be 'chosen' in the biblical sense of that word . . . charged with a special responsibility, *an obligation* . . . to realize, as best [we] can . . . a higher law." See his book, *The Constitution, the Courts, and Human Rights* (New Haven: Yale University Press, 1982), pp. 97, 98. Although this constitutional vision may comport well with the Puritans' and other early Americans' self-understandings, it is emphatically *not* nonsectarian; it betrays a yearning for an essentialist politics congenial to the traditional moral understandings that presumably are shared by the majority of Americans. Perry's earlier essay, "Substantive Due Process Revisited: Reflections on (And Beyond) Recent Cases," *Northwestern University Law Review* 71, no. 4 (September–October 1976): 417–469, proposes that the role of the Court is to represent the public's conventional morality so as to maintain its legitimacy. Also see Mark A. Noll, "The Constitution at 200: Should Christians Join the Celebration?" *Christianity Today* 31, no. 9 (July 10, 1987): 18–23, which proposes that the Constitution reflects a Christian ethos and is subservient to the "Kingdom of God."

19. For example, constitutional scholar Stephen E. Gottlieb argues in his book, *Morality Imposed: The Rehnquist Court and Liberty in America* (New York: New York University Press, 2000), pp. 30–31, 68, that the *Bowers* case is emblematic of this morals discourse, one unconnected to any objectively verifiable showing of harm to others, and also a characteristic attitude of the archconservative minority on the Rehnquist Court.
20. See Walter Barnett, "Corruption of Morals—The Underlying Issue of the Pornography Commission Report," *Arizona State University Law Journal*, vol. 1971: 222–223. For a contrasting view, see Gary L. Young, Jr., "The Price of Public Endorsement: A Reply to Mr. Marcosson," *UMKC Law Review* 64, no. 1 (Fall 1995), 99–115. Young writes: "Let us make the stakes clear: *the people who object to the recognition of open homosexuality in the military do so because they want to maintain the general societal commitment that homosexuality is a morally objectionable lifestyle.*" See Ibid., 107 (emphasis original).
21. Romer v. Evans, 116 S.Ct. 1620, 1627, 1628, 1629 (1996) (Kennedy, J., opinion of the Court).
22. See G. Sidney Buchanan, "Same-Sex Marriage: The Linchpin Issue," *University of Dayton Law Review* 10, no. 3 (Spring 1985): 541–573.
23. Ibid., 562.
24. One response both to Buchanan's thesis and to Perry's look to conventional morality is provided by Joel Feinberg, "Legal Moralism and Freefloating Evils," *Pacific Philosophical Quarterly* 61, nos. 1 & 2 (January–April 1980): 122–155, who categorizes and assesses a great variety of purported harms and offenses to the moral climate that are often taken to merit criminal sanction, but cannot legitimately receive any such sanction.
25. On the enduring Christian intolerance and frequent animosity towards homosexual behavior and, later, gay persons, at least in some prominent denominations down through the centuries, see Derrick Sherwin Bailey, *Homosexuality and the Western Christian Tradition* (London: Longmans, Green and Co, 1955), which shows that there has been no significant alteration since the end of the Middle Ages, as well as an overriding concern for warding off God's wrath as per Sodom; and Reverend Ellen M. Barrett, "Legal Homophobia and the Christian Church," *Hastings Law Journal* 30, no. 4 (March 1979): 1019–1027, which discusses homosexuality's role in the historical power struggle between church and state in England.
26. See Goody, *The development of the family and marriage in Europe*, pp. 77, 221.
27. Here, historical sweep and the perspective of minority groups are usefully consulted. For example, see Forrest G. Wood, *The Arrogance of Faith: Christianity & Race in America from the Colonial Era to the Twentieth Century* (Boston: Northeastern University Press, 1990), which details historical Christian support for extermination of Native American Indians, and the biblical defenses of slavery and conquest. Also see William P. Marshall, "The Other Side of Religion," *Hastings Law Journal* 44, no. 4 (April 1993): 843–863.
28. Religion is the explicit topic of Chapter Twelve in Hobbes' masterwork, *Leviathan*, originally published in 1651.
29. See Ted G. Jelen, "In Defense of Religious Minimalism," in Mary C. Segers and Ted G. Jelen, *A Wall of Separation?: Debating the Public Role of Religion* (Lanham: Rowman & Littlefield, 1998).

30. See Gerald F. Gaus, *Justificatory Liberalism: An Essay on Epistemology and Political Theory* (Oxford: Oxford University Press, 1996), pp. 170, 171.
31. See David A. J. Richards, *Women, Gays, and the Constitution,* pp. 41–42, 44–45, 46.
32. See Dennis Prager, "Homosexuality, the Bible, and us – a Jewish Perspective," *Public Interest* No. 112 (Summer 1993): 66, 72, 82.
33. See Henkin, 'Morals and the Constitution,' 411, 407. The origins in religious authority of the heterosexual marriage union is made explicit in John R. W. Stott, "Homosexual 'Marriage': Why same-sex partnerships are not a Christian option," *Christianity Today* 29, no. 17 (November 22, 1985): 21–28.
34. *Barnes v. Glen Theatre, Inc.*, 111 S.Ct. 2456, 2465 (1991) (Scalia, J., concurring in the judgment). The notion that the Court should function as the *custos morum* has a long history, and was well-expressed in Lord Mansfield's dictum of 1774: "Whatever is *contra bonos mores et decorum* the principles of our laws prohibit and the King's Court as the general censor and guardian of the public morals is bound to restrain and punish." Quoted in H.L.A. Hart, *Law, Liberty, and Morality* (Stanford: Stanford University Press, 1963), p. 7. The Bill of Rights of the United States Constitution stands opposed to this enlarged perspective as to the legitimate purview of the State.
35. See John Rawls, *Political Liberalism* (New York: Columbia University Press, 1993), p. 41.

Chapter Four. Professor Richards Finds a Violation

1. American freedom fighter Thomas Paine, quoted in Jack Nicholas, *The Gay Agenda: Talking Back to the Fundamentalists* (Amherst: Prometheus Books, 1996), p. 35.
2. Richards, "Sexual Preference as a Suspect (Religious) Classification," 550.
3. Regarding Locke, see Jeremy Waldron, "Locke: toleration and the rationality of persecution," in Susan Mendus, ed., *Justifying Toleration: Conceptual and Historical Perspectives* (Cambridge: Cambridge University Press, 1988), pp. 61–86, dissecting Locke's argument that intolerance and persecution are "rationally inappropriate" and imprudent, yet not wrong. A good presentation of the evolution of liberty of conscience in thought during the pivotal sixteenth and seventeenth centuries is John Plamenatz, *Man and Society: A Critical Examination of Some Important Social and Political Theories from Machiavelli to Marx,* Volume One (London: Longman's, 1963), pp. 45–88. The kindred progression from rule by custom and "higher law" to rule by legitimate civil authority in the constitutionally ordered republic is treated in Howell A. Lloyd, "Constitutionalism," in J. H. Burns, ed., *The Cambridge History of Political Thought 1450–1700* (Cambridge: Cambridge University Press, 1991), pp. 254–297.
4. See Brian Barry, *Justice as Impartiality* (Oxford: Clarendon Press, 1995), pp. 163–164.
5. See Joseph Charles Heim, "The Demise of the Confessional State and the Rise of the Idea of a Legitimate Minority," in John W. Chapman and Alan Wertheimer, eds., *NOMOS XXXII. Majorities and Minorities* (New York: New York University Press, 1990), pp. 19, 20.

6. The religion clauses are said to have been incorporated into the states through the Fourteenth Amendment in the Court cases of Cantwell v. Connecticut (310 U.S. 296 [1940]) and Everson v. Board of Education (330 U.S. 1 [1947]).
7. This understanding of the meaning of the Establishment Clause is taken from constitutional scholar Leonard W. Levy. See his essay, "The Original Meaning of the Establishment Clause," in *Constitutional Opinions: Aspects of the Bill of Rights* (New York: Oxford University Press, 1986), pp. 135–161; and his book, *The Establishment Clause: Religion and the First Amendment,* Second Edition, Revised (Chapel Hill: University of North Carolina Press, 1994). The following references convey the same understanding. For a history of the discussion on religious liberty, so-called nonpreferentialism, and other topics from the colonial period through the eighteenth century, see Thomas J. Curry, *The First Freedoms: Church and State in America to the Passage of the First Amendment* (New York: Oxford University Press, 1986). An accessible treatment of the creation of, and rationale supporting a "godless constitution," and the history of repudiated major challenges thereto is given in Isaac Kramnick and R. Laurence Moore, *The Godless Constitution: The Case Against Religious Correctness* (New York: W.W. Norton, 1996). Also see Joseph L. Blau, ed., *Cornerstones of Religious Freedom in America,* Revised and Enlarged Edition (New York: Harper & Row, 1964).
8. See Diana L. Eck, *A New Religious America: How a "Christian Country" Has Become the World's Most Religiously Diverse Nation* (San Francisco: Harper-Collins, 2001), pp. 41, 384. Eck also argues for the intended "godlessness" of the Constitution, and for the United States' disestablishment of "even Christianity itself," in Ibid., p. 42.
9. Richards, "Sexual Preference as a Suspect (Religious) Classification," 550. One law review essay applies the analytical framework developed by Richards to anti-gay initiatives. See Marc L. Rubenstein, "NOTE: Gay Rights and Religion: A Doctrinal Approach to the Argument that Anti-Gay Rights Initiatives Violate the Establishment Clause," *Hastings Law Journal* 46 (July 1995). Rubenstein's focus is anti-gay rights initiatives as violating the Establishment Clause, primarily because of the religious motivation of their supporters who have an abiding antipathy towards homosexuality, if not also against gay persons. As mentioned earlier, the argument philosophically closest to that of this book is Wenz, Abortion Rights as *Religious Freedom*. An argument similiar to Richards' has been made, but in the context of a broader analysis of establishment clause jurisprudence in three other areas of morality legislation. See Sherryle E. Michaelson, "Note. Religion and Morality Legislation: A Reexamination of Establishment Clause Analysis," *New York University Law Review* 59, no. 2 (May 1984): 301–409. Similarly, in the course of making a point about justice inspiring impartiality with respect to understanding the good of mature sexual expression, one scholar analogizes to a freedom of sexual expression, arguing that this freedom and freedom of religious worship are constitutionally parallel. See Barry, *Justice as Impartiality*, pp. 83–85, 143.
10. Richards, "Sexual Preference as a Suspect (Religious) Classification," 493.
11. Ibid., 495, 499, 547–550.

12. Richards, "Sexual Preference as a Suspect (Religious) Classification," 495–496, 499.
13. Ibid., 521.
14. Richards, "Sexual Preference as a Suspect (Religious) Classification," 521–522.
15. Ibid., 522–523.
16. Richards, "Sexual Preference as a Suspect (Religious) Classification," 547, 552.
17. Ibid., 524, 539, 545.
18. Richards, "Sexual Preference as a Suspect (Religious) Classification," 493.
19. See Martha Shelley's essay, "Gay is Good," reprinted in Mark Blasius and Shane Phelan, eds., *We Are Everywhere: A Historical Sourcebook of Gay and Lesbian Politics* (New York: Routledge, 1997 [orig. 1970]), pp. 391–393.
20. See Richards, *Women, Gays and the Constitution*, p. 356.
21. See the discussion of ethical living in Mark Blasius, *Gay and Lesbian Politics: Sexuality and the Emergence of a New Ethic* (Philadelphia: Temple University Press, 1994). Richards makes the important connection in ethics between the constitutional liberty of conscience and moral self-government in his earlier essay "Religion, Public Morality, and Constitutional Law," in J. Roland Pennock and John W. Chapman, eds., *NOMOS XXX. Religion, Morality, and the Law* (New York: New York University Press, 1988), pp. 152–178.
22. Richards, "Sexual Preference as a Suspect (Religious) Classification," 493–494.
23. The First Amendment's religion clauses apply as well to expression of deeply-held, sincere, and meaningful *nonreligious* beliefs distinguished by the absence of a relation to a supreme being. Nontheistic, conscientious conviction that disavows religious belief is constitutionally protected, even against conscription. See *United States v. Seeger*, 380 U.S. 163 (1965); affirmed in *Welsh v. United States*, 398 U.S. 333 (1970). Also see the discussion in David McKenzie, "The Supreme Court, Fundamentalist Logic, and the Term 'Religion,'" *Journal of Church and State* 33, no. 4 (Autumn 1991): 731–746.
24. Richards, "Sexual Preference as a Suspect (Religious) Classification," 508, 499, 509.
25. See Keller, "Divining the Priest," 514.
26. Or, in Richards' words:

    If political homophobia is, on examination, constitutionally illegitimate expression of religious intolerance, public laws reflecting this prejudice should be forthrightly constitutionally suspect on the clearest textual and historical constitutional grounds: the central American constitutional tradition of religious toleration under the religion clauses of the First Amendment that suspect classification analysis under the Equal Protection Clause of the Fourteenth Amendment assumes and elaborates, and certainly does not repeal or retrench.

    See Richards, "Sexual Preference as a Suspect (Religious) Classification," 506.
27. See Tinsley E. Yarbrough, "Church, State, and the Rehnquist Court: A Brief for Lemon," *Journal of Church and State* 38, no. 1 (Winter 1996): 59–85. Yarbrough argues that nonpreferentialism is inconsistent with our constitutional regime, and that it fails the Court's Lemon test for establishment. See Ibid., 84–85.
28. See Levy, *The Establishment Clause*, pp. 153–154.
29. Ibid., pp. 241–242.

Part III. How to Identify Sub Rosa *Establishment and the Argument by Definition*

1. See James E. Wood, Jr., "No Religious Test Shall Ever Be Required": Reflections on the Bicentennial of the U.S. Constitution," *Journal of Church and State* 29, no. 2 (Spring 1987): 200, 201, 206–207.
2. For example, "We atheists, doing our best to enforce Jefferson's compromise, think it bad enough that we cannot run for public office without being disingenuous about our disbelief in God; despite the compromise, no unclosetcd atheist is likely to get elected anywhere in the country." See Richard Rorty, "Religion As Conversation-Stopper," *Common Knowledge* 3, no. 1 (Spring 1994): 2.
3. See Arthur Hertzberg, "The Protestant 'Establishment,' Catholic Dogma, & the Presidency," *Commentary* 30, no. 4 (October 1960): 277–285.
4. See Stephen M. Feldman, *Please Don't Wish Me a Merry Christmas: A Critical History of the Separation of Church and State* (New York: New York University Press, 1997), p. 161. Also see the discussion of the *de facto* Protestant establishment and the Fourteenth Amendment in Thomas C. Berg, *The State and Religion. In a Nutshell* (St. Paul: West Group, 1998), pp. 56–62.
5. Maryland's Constitution once contained an explicit violation of this clause; it required a declaration by would-be public office holders of their belief in God. This provision was struck down by the Supreme Court in Torasco v. Watkins (367 U.S. 488 [1961]). At issue was an established nonpreferential (i.e., nondenominational) preference in the law for believers, burdening nonbelievers.
6. 367 U.S. 488, 495 (1961) (reference notes omitted).
7. Perez v. Lippold, 198 P.2d 17, 19, 20, 21 (California, 1948) (emphasis added).
8. *Loving v. Virginia*, 388 U.S. 1, 12 (1966) (emphasis added).
9. Regarding this alternative thesis, see Keller, "Divining the Priest," 504, 525–526.
10. For particularly illuminating treatments of the issue of the law's real target in this type of morals legislation, see Janet E. Halley, "Reasoning about Sodomy: Act and Identity In and After *Bowers v. Hardwick*," *Virginia Law Review* 79, no. 7 (October 1993): 1721–1780, which argues that the real target is sexual-orientation identity, and that the act/identity relationship is in reality highly, though usefully unstable; and, Nan D. Hunter, "Life After *Hardwick*," *Harvard Civil Rights-Civil Liberties Law Review* 27, no. 2 (Summer 1992): 531–554. Also see Joseph R. Gusfield, "On Legislating Morals: The Symbolic Process of Designating Deviance," *California Law Review* 56, no. 1 (January 1968): 54–73, which argues that the presumed consensus supporting morals legislation is tenuous, that hostility is embedded in law, the effect of which is "domination without legitimacy".
11. The highly problematical issue of "naked preferences" escaping constitutional filters and finding their way into public law is ably presented in Cass R. Sunstein, "Preferences and Politics," *Philosophy & Public Affairs* 20, no. 1 (Winter 1991): 4–34.

Chapter Five. The Shadow Establishment *Has Its Day in Court*

1. For quick background information on these as well as other church-state cases, see the table of Supreme Court decisions in Wayne R. Swanson, *The Christ Child Goes to Court* (Philadelphia: Temple University Press, 1990), pp. 51–52, Table I. The history of Supreme Court jurisprudence in this area is discussed in Frederick Mark Gedicks, *The Rhetoric of Church and State: A Critical Analysis of Religion Clause Jurisprudence* (Durham: Duke University Press, 1995); and, Phillip E. Hammond, *With Liberty for All: Freedom of Religion in the United States* (Louisville: Westminster John Knox Press, 1998).
2. 333 U.S. 203, 210, 212 (1948), quoting from *Everson v. Board of Education*, 330 U.S. 1 (1946), where the justices were unanimous regarding separation of church and state, and the metaphor of the wall and the value of neutrality were inscribed in the law. That *Everson* unanimously incorporated the strict separation view of the Establishment Clause was affirmed in *Lee v. Weisman*, 112 S.Ct. 2649, 2673, n.4 (1992) (Souter, J., concurring opinion). Souter's concurring opinion in *Lee* gives perhaps the best most recent statement by the Court regarding nonpreferential state promotion of religion, considered to be a misguided thesis that is unconstitutional in practice and carries with it grave implications touching citizenship, settled law, and free exercise of religion. Id. at 2667–2678.
3. 333 U.S. 203, 209 (1948).
4. *Id.* at 255–256 (Reed, J., dissenting).
5. 333 U.S. 203, 249 (1948) (Reed, J., dissenting).
6. *Id.* at 227, 231, 232 (Frankfurter, J., concurring) (references omitted) (emphasis added). People from across the political spectrum can safely affirm strict separation, as these words from Republican Senator Arlen Specter demonstrate:

    When we create the fact, *or even just the perception,* that the instruments of government are being used to support one person's faith and not another's, we make the citizenship of some people just a little less valuable that the citizenship of others. And, in doing that, we risk the fabric of toleration that permits our nation of diverse people and different creeds to thrive as one.

    See Arlen Specter, "Defending the Wall: Maintaining Church/State Separation in America," *Harvard Journal of Law & Public Policy* 18, no. 2 (Spring 1995): 586 (emphasis added).
7. See Milton R. Konvitz, "Separation of Church and State: The First Freedom," *Law and Contemporary Problems* 14 (Winter 1949): 44, 45, where this point-of-view is discussed.
8. Ibid., 47, 48. Also see Leonard W. Levy, *Original Intent and the Framers' Constitution* (New York: Macmillan, 1988), pp. 178–180, which argues that government has no authority to legislate on the subject of religion, a "forbidden field."
9. See the discussion of Madison as a Virginia legislator contributing to the debates of the day surrounding church and state, culminating in his *Memorial and Remonstrance Against Religious Assessments* in Irving Brant, *James Madison. The Nationalist, 1780–1787* (Indianapolis: Bobbs-Merrill, 1948), pp. 343–355 (quoted passages on pp. 344, 351).

134   LIBERAL CONSTITUTIONALISM

10. 343 U.S. 306, 310, 312, 313 (1952) (Douglas, J. opinion of the Court).
11. *Id.* at 314.
12. 343 U.S. 306, 313–314 (1952) (emphasis added).
13. This view expressed in *Zorach* is mistaken and historically inaccurate, or so it is argued in Douglas Laycock, "'Nonpreferential' Aid to Religion: A False Claim about Original Intent," William and Mary Law Review 27 (1986): 875–923.
14. 343 U.S. 306, 318 (1952) (Black, J., dissenting).
15. *Id.* at 319, 320.
16. 330 U.S. 1, 16 (1947) (Black, J., opinion of the Court).
17. 343 U.S. 306, 324, 325 (1952) (Jackson, J., dissenting).
18. The reader is recommended to consult the comprehensive treatment of Sunday Closing "blue laws" by Andrew J. King, "Sunday Law in the Nineteenth Century," Albany Law Review 64 (2000). King writes of the great variety of cases that were litigated in court, that "[w]hile many of these decisions were disingenuous or ambiguous about their religious roots, their explicit secular basis allowed the courts to use a secular yardstick to measure the offensiveness of Sunday contracts." See Ibid., 710. Our concern here is to challenge that secular basis, which we view as a fig leaf.
19. Nonetheless, some past historical figures have attempted just that, to demonstrate the objectivity and accuracy of Biblical accounts, as in the following humorous example of pinpointing the very moment of "creation":

    Irish Bishop James Ussher (1581–1656) wrote a chronology of the Old Testament, in which he added up all the generations of men and women mentioned in the Bible since Adam and Eve, and pegged Creation at 4004 B.C., at 2:30 p.m., Sunday, October 23! One person is said to have asked the bishop, "And pray, Holy Father, what was God doing *before* he created the universe?" To which Ussher replied impatiently, "Creating hell for those who ask such questions!"

    See David Eliot Brody and Arnold R. Brody, The Science Class You Wish You Had (New York: Perigree/Berkley Publishing Group, 1997), p. 153 (emphasis original). I am indebted to my colleague Dr. Anuradha Prakash, Chair of Chapman University's Department of the Physical Sciences, for this reference.
20. 366 U.S. 420, 431 (1960).
21. *Id.* at 431, 444.
22. 366 U.S. 420, 445 (1960). The section also used the terms "Lord's day" and "Sabbath day," terms that indicate sacred obligations and institutions, and a vocabulary inseparable from traditional American Christianity.
23. *Id.* at 442. At one point in his concurring opinion Justice Frankfurter practically repeated this passage, though his examples of legitimate regulations in coincidence with tenets of faith were usury and monogamy. *Id.* at 462 (Frankfurter, J., concurring opinion).
24. 366 U.S. 420, 445 (1960).
25. *Id.* at 448–449.
26. 366 U.S. 420, 450 (1960).
27. *Id.* at 420 (from the case Syllabus).
28. 366 U.S. 420, 452 (1960) (references omitted) (emphasis added).
29. The lineage of these laws extends back to a time when their religious nature

30. 366 U.S. 420, 461–462 (1960) (Frankfurter, J., concurring opinion).
31. Id. at 466–467. Justice Frankfurter's test is no longer used, having been replaced with the three-pronged *Lemon* test, which also requires a secular purpose (*Lemon v. Kurtzman*, 403 U.S. 602 [1971]). Here, we are interested in illustrative lines of reasoning that surround the shadow establishment, and so will not investigate the latter test. But, see Michaelson, "Note. Religion and Morality Legislation," 309–311, arguing that the ban on same-sex marriage fails the *Lemon* test.
32. 366 U.S. 420, 565 (1960) (Douglas, J., dissenting). Douglas also asked about a secular day of rest on another day, one that corresponded with, say, Moslem scruples? Id. at 576.
33. 366 U.S. 420, 564 (1960) (Douglas, J., dissenting).
34. Id. at 561, 563.
35. 366 U.S. 420, 569 (1960) (Douglas, J., dissenting).
36. See King, "Sunday Law in the Nineteenth Century," p. 678.
37. 366 U.S. 420, 576, n.7 (1960).
38. In *Braunfeld*, decided the following year, the Court, relying on *McGowan*, upheld the Sunday Closing Law at issue, acknowledged the economic burden on minority faiths, but then effaced the economic issue in the following way: "To allow people who rest on a day other than Sunday to keep their businesses open on that day might well provide these people with an economic advantage over their competitors who must remain closed on that day; this might cause the Sunday-observers to complain that their religion are being discriminated against." *Braunfeld et al. v. Brown*, 366 U.S. 599, 602 (1961) (Warren, C.J., opinion of the Court) (references omitted). The animating concern implied here is, the freedom of religious expression of mainstream Christian faiths should be accommodated without burdening them economically, even though their competitors may be so burdened by this accommodation. The dissenting opinions by Justices Brennan and Stewart are reminiscent of Justice Douglas' in *McGowan*, who offered his dissent from that earlier case here as well.
39. 366 U.S. 420, 575 (1960) (Douglas, J., dissenting).
40. Id. at 572–573. The possibility of a disingenuous secular rationale existing alongside a religious motivation is underappreciated by Rubenstein, who is persuaded that the Sunday Closing law in *McGowan* is sufficiently secular and well-tailored, and no longer religious. See Rubenstein, "NOTE: Gay Rights and Religion," 1612–1614.
41. See the discussion of the First Amendment in Chapter Four.
42. Without the religious dimension antecedently imbuing marriage with its meaning, marriage would be regarded by the state as just another contract between two adults, save for the spouses' purposes. See John Dwight Ingram, "A Constitutional Critique of Restrictions on the Right to Marry—Why Can't Fred Marry George – Or Mary and Alice at the Same Time?" *Journal of Contemporary Law* 10 (1984): 33–55.

Chapter Six. A Note Regarding the Appeal to the Dictionary

1. Cases of same-sex marriage in the courts are discussed in Chapter Eight.
2. One legal reference work puts the point this way: "*Webster's*, however, is not necessarily concerned with the question whether a particular usage is constitutionally objectionable, or even discriminatory." See Walter O. Weyrauch and Sanford N. Katz, *American Family Law in Transition* (Washington: Bureau of National Affairs, Inc., 1983), p. 430.
3. See Mark Strasser, "Domestic Relations Jurisprudence and the Great, Slumbering *Baehr:* On Definitional Preclusion, Equal Protection, and Fundamental Interests," *Fordham Law Review* 64 (December 1995): 926, 927.
4. See the discussion of non-obvious meanings and dictionary entries in Mary E. Hunt, "Too Sexy for Words: The Changing Vocabulary of Religious Ethics," Chapter Eight in Sands, ed., *God Forbid*.
5. For example, in *Dean v. District of Columbia* (653 A.2d. 307 [D.C. 1992]), the Court denied a same-sex couple a marriage license because of the definition of marriage, but used "biblical references to determine the common usage and understanding of the term 'marriage.' Reported in the Recent Developments section of the University of Hawai'i Law Review, "For Better or for Worse, in Sickness and in Health, Until Death Do Us Part: A Look at Same-Sex Marriage in Hawaii," *University of Hawai'i Law Review* 16, no. 1 (Summer 1994): 460, n.95.
6. See the examples of dictionary definitions of marriage that do not simply mention it as an opposite-sex institution, and the discussion of the "oxymoronic objection" in Eskridge, *The Case for Same-Sex Marriage*, pp. 89–104.
7. See Silverstein, "Comment. Constitutional Aspects of the Homosexual's Right to a Marriage License," 619, n.46.
8. And even in the realm of biblical connotations, there is so much to interrogate that one despairs of finding a solid biblical basis for a legal ruling, despite the invocations of biblical authority, which must be unrecognized in American courts anyway. On the matter of clarity and coherence in the vocabulary of Christian biblical traditions, see Jordan, *The Invention of Sodomy in Christian Theology*.
9. Dawson v. Vance, 329 F.Supp. 1320, 1322 (1971) (emphasis added). Court cases involving "gay marriage" are discussed more fully in Chapter Eight.
10. *Doe v. Commonwealth's Atty. for the City of Richmond*, 403 F.Supp. 1199, 1202 (1975) (emphasis added).
11. See her essay, "Leviticus in America: The Politics of Sex Crimes," *Journal of Political Philosophy* 1, no. 1 (1993): 105–136.
12. See Lewis, "From This Day Forward," p. 1783, criticizing the institution of marriage for being "an exclusive privilege conditioned upon heterosexual orientation" such that the "definitional equation of marriage with heterosexuality forms a self-enclosed system inaccessible to single-gender couples who desire equal protection under the law for their intimate enduring relationships."
13. See the discussion of the negatively valenced sex vocabulary and appropriate constitutional discourse in Chapter Three.
14. The denominations currently allowing for same-sex marriage include Unitar-

ians, Episcopalians, United Church of Christ, Reform Judaism, and the Society of Friends (or, Quakers). This list is not likely to grow any shorter, and may soon include Methodists and Presbyterians.
15. See the religion-contextualized discussion of the meaning of marriage as a lifestyle and journey in Evelyn Eaton Whitehead and James D. Whitehead, "The Meaning of Marriage" and "Marriage Becomes a Journey," Chapters Nine and Ten in Scott and Warren, eds., *Perspectives on Marriage.*
16. Across the United States same-sex marriage and other contemporary issues relating to sexuality and family life being played out at the level of the local church. See Keith Hartman, *Congregations in Conflict: The Battle Over Homosexuality* (New Brunswick: Rutgers University Press, 1996), for a compelling introduction to the nature of these discussions, and the passions and sympathies of ordinary Americans grappling with their faith tradition and their love of neighbor.
17. Boaz, *Libertarianism: A Primer,* pp. 241–242.

Part IV. The Shadow Establishment, "Gay Marriage" in the Courts, and the Analogies to Race and Polygamy

1. *Bradwell v. Illinois,* 21 L.Ed 442, 446 (1873) (Bradley, J., concurring opinion). *Bradwell* concerned whether Illinois' regulation against admitting women to the state bar was constitutional. Justice Bradley opined that the regulation was within the police powers of the state, "in view of the peculiar characteristics, destiny, and mission of woman." See *Id.*
2. See L. William Countryman, "The Bible, Heterosexism, and the American Public Discussion of Sexual Orientation," Chapter Nine in Sands, ed., *God Forbid,* pp. 167, 170, 171.
3. For example, see Sheldon H. Nahmod, "The Public Square and the Jew as Religious Other," *Hastings Law Journal* 44, no. 4 (April 1993): 865–870. The significance of these differences for political theory (e.g., Jewish emphasis on Talmudic law, long historical experience, and the rabbinic tradition) can be gleamed from many of the essays collected in Daniel H. Frank, ed., *Commandment and Community: New Essays in Jewish Legal and Political Philosophy* (Albany: State University of New York Press, 1995).
4. See B. Carmon Hardy, *Solemn Covenant: The Mormon Polygamous Passage* (Urbana: University of Illinois Press, 1992), pp. 40, 41, 60.
5. Legal historian Hendrik Hartog presents the multiple regimes of American marriage, and the variety of relationships people have taken in the face of legal descriptions that would have them behave otherwise, with all of this being quite normal at the end of the day, in his book, *Man and Wife in America: A History* (Cambridge: Harvard University Press, 2000).

Chapter Seven. Interracial and Plural Marriage Analogies and Cases

1. See the fine law review essays by Daniel R. Gordon, "The Ugly Mirror: *Bowers, Plessy* and the Reemergence of the Constitutionalism of Social Stratification and Historical Reinforcement," *Journal of Contemporary Law* 19, no. 1 (1993): 21–50; Andrew Koppelman, "The Miscegenation Analogy: Sodomy Law as Sex Discrimination," *Yale Law Journal* 98, no. 1 (November 1988): 145–164; Mark Strasser, "Family, Definitions, and the Constitution: On the Miscegenation Analogy," *Suffolk University Law Review* 25, no. 4 (Winter 1991): 981–1034; and, Robert F. Drinan, "The Loving Decision and the Freedom to Marry," *Ohio State Law Journal* 29 (1968): 358–398.
2. See Robert J. Sickels, *Race, Marriage and the Law* (Albuquerque: University of New Mexico Press, 1972), pp. 8, 13, 10–19.
3. See Rachel F. Moran, *Interracial Intimacy: The Regulation of Race & Romance* (Chicago: University of Chicago Press, 2001). Moran includes in her book discussions of "lovableness," autonomy, and the history of the perceived moral impropriety of "separate but equal families," with express implications for the pursuit of equality throughout the nation's many communities still separated by a dearth of interracial, personal relationships.
4. There have been laws affecting the marriage and family relationships between whites and non-whites in 38 states. Reported in Moran, *Interracial Intimacy*, p. 17.
5. Karen M. Woods, in her law review essay "Law Making: A 'Wicked and Mischievous Connection': The Origins of Indian-White Miscegenation Law," *Legal Studies Forum* 23 (1999), discusses the popularity of miscegenation laws in early America, as well as their use in Native American Indian cultures to prevent dilution of their race.
6. See Moran, *Interracial Intimacy*, p. 18.
7. See Sunstein's thoughtful law review essay, "Homosexuality and the Constitution," which expounds on the miscegenation analogy to gay marriage.
8. See Andrew Koppelman, *Antidiscrimination Law and Social Equality* (New Haven: Yale University Press, 1996), pp. 153–154.
9. Quoted in the Opinion of the Court in *Loving v. Virginia*, 388 U.S. 1, 3 (1966).
10. See Woods, "Law Making," discussing the marriage of Pocahontas and the Christian religious motivation behind early miscegenation statutes.
11. 198 P.2d 17, 35, 37, 40, 41 (1948) (Shenk, J., dissenting) (citations omitted).
12. See Drinan, "The Loving Decision and the Freedom to Marry," 363.
13. Ibid., 360, 364.
14. See J. Harvie Wilkinson III and G. Edward White, "Constitutional Protection for Personal Lifestyles," *Cornell Law Review* 62, no. 3 (March 1977): 573–574, an essay unsupportive of same-sex relationships.
15. See Richard F. Duncan, "From Loving to Romer: Homosexual Marriage and Moral Discernment," *Brigham Young University Journal of Public Law* 12(1998): 251.
16. See Ibid., p. 239. Graff reports that the decision in *Loving* was not popular, as 72% of those polled by Gallup disapproved of interracial marriage—"far more than disapprove of same-sex marriage today"—and 48% believed it should be a crime. See Graff, *What Is Marriage For?*, p. 156.

17. The connection between family law, sexuality, and autonomy is pursued throughout Moran, *Interracial Intimacy*, esp. Chapter four.
18. This line of reasoning about religiously-based racism morphing into one or other strand of scientific endeavour is taken from Keith E. Sealing, "Blood Will Tell: Scientific Racism and the Legal Prohibition Against Miscegenation," *Michigan Journal of Race and Law* 5 (Spring 2000).
19. For background information on the practice of plural marriage outside of the Mormon context, consult the following sources. Blu Greenberg, "Marriage in the Jewish Tradition," Chapter Thirty-six in Scott and Warren, eds., *Perspectives on Marriage*; Rebecca T. Alpert, "Religious Liberty, Same-Sex Marriage, and the Case of Reconstructionist Judaism," Chapter Six in Sands, ed., *God Forbid* (arguing for freedom of religious expression to marry same-sex couples, as is the contemporary practice in this tradition, but with legal recognition); Lois Lamya' Ibsen al Faruqi, "Marriage in Islam," Chapter Thirty-eight in Scott and Warren, eds., *Perspectives on Marriage* (discussing that while marriage was declared a sacrament in Christianity in the twelfth century, it is not regarded as a sacrament in Islam); Eugene Hillman, *Polygamy Reconsidered: African plural marriage and the Christian Churches* (Maryknoll, New York: Orbis Books, 1975); and, Philip L. Kilbride, *Plural Marriage for Our Times: A Reinvented Option?* (Westport: Bergin & Garvey, 1994) (critiques Eurocentric bias as a hindrance to realization of the diversity in marriage relationships). American courts have also heard cases involving the plural marriages of non-Mormons (e.g., *Sharma v. Sharma*, 667 P.2d 395 [Kan.App. 1983]). The earlier case of *Singh v. Boyes*, 83 Cal. App. 2d 256 (1948), briefly reviews prior North American cases involving plural and interracial marriages.
20. For example, see Jan Shipps, "Beyond the Stereotypes: Mormon and Non-Mormon Communities in Twentieth-Century Mormondom," in Davis Bitton and Maureen Ursenbach Beecher, eds., *New Views of Mormon History. A Collection of Essays in Honor of Leonard J. Arrington* (Salt Lake City: University of Utah Press, 1987), pp. 342–362. For background sources on the Church of Jesus Christ of Latter-day Saints, or Mormonism, a peculiarly American religion, see the now classic book by Kimball Young, *Isn't One Wife Enough?* (New York: Henry Holt, 1954); and, the study of the limitations of a reactionary American religious and social pluralism in Marvin S. Hill, *Quest for Refuge: The Mormon Flight from American Pluralism* (Salt Lake City: Signature Books, 1989).
21. An overall similiar approach was taken in an argument limited to overcoming the ban on bigamous or polygamous marriage. See G. Keith Nedrow, "Polygamy and the Right to Marry: New Life for an Old Lifestyle," *Memphis State University Law Review* 11, no. 3 (Spring 1981): 303–349.
22. *Reynolds v. United States*, 25 L.Ed. 244, 250 (1879). *Reynolds* stands for the principle that religion *simpliciter* provides no cover for illegal acts, regardless of the level of harm to others involved.
23. *Id.* at 250.
24. That the Mormon belief was sincere was never in doubt in *Reynolds*. See Hardy, *Solemn Covenant*, Chapter 1, for a discussion of the principled basis of plural or "celestial" marriage in Mormon teaching. Polygamy, nonetheless, was not the practice of all, or even most, Mormons. See Stanley S. Ivins,

140 LIBERAL CONSTITUTIONALISM

"Notes on Mormon Polygamy," reprinted in Marvin S. Hill and James B. Allen, eds., *Mormonism and American Culture* (New York: Harper & Row, 1972), pp. 101–111. We are going to ignore the many other features of this nineteenth-century debate so as to focus attention on the conflict between normative regimes. Other features of the context include the precious metal silver, the politics of westward expansion, the property of the Mormon Church and its power in the Utah Territory, contemporary fascination with exotic sexual practices such as "Mormon aberrance," and the emerging women's movement, then waging a campaign against the oppression of women thought inherent to polygamous marriage. On the latter points, see Sarah Barringer Gordon, "Our National Hearthstone: Anti-Polygamy Fiction and the Sentimental Campaign Against Moral Diversity in Antebellum America," *Yale Journal of Law and the Humanities* 8, no. 2 (Summer 1996), who argues that monogamous marriage became ideologized as the basis of civilization in the process of the political campaign against the Mormons. Bigamy and polygamy cases are discussed in Schombert, "*Baehr v. Lewin:* How Far Has the Door Been Opened?," 335–336.

25. 29 L.Ed. 47, 57–58 (1884).
26. 33 L.Ed. 637, 639, 640 (1890). Placing polygamy outside the bounds of "serious discussion" evokes Devlin's mention of the disutility in opening up for debate the Christian idea of marriage submerged in the marital regime of England, as discussed in Chapter Three.
27. See John Stuart Mill, *On Liberty* (New York: Prometheus, 1986 [orig. 1859]), pp. 103–104.
28. *Late Corporation of Latter-day Saints and Romney v. United States,* 34 L.Ed. 478, 493, 494 (1890) (emphasis added). "Extirpation" of polygamy and "escheating" the Mormon Church were two important steps in the process towards statehood for Utah. See Howard R. Lamar, "Statehood for Utah: A Different Path," reprinted in Hill and Allen, *Mormonism and American Culture,* pp. 127–141.
29. The relevant cases are: *Cleveland v. United States,* 329 U.S. 14 (1946); *Musser v. Utah,* 333 U.S. 95 (1948); and, the two *Potter v. Murray City* cases, at 585 F.Supp. 1126 (1984), and 760 F.2d 1065 (1985).
30. *In the Matter of the Adoption of . . . v. Vaughn Fischer and Sharane Fischer,* 808 P.2d 1083, 1085 (Utah 1991). The trial court's denial of adoption into a polygamous family was overturned.
31. The Latter-day Saints, officially, condemn homosexuality and have donated considerable sums of money to anti-same-sex marriage initiatives in several states. See Richard N. Ostling and Joan K. Ostling, *Mormon America: The Power and the Promise* (San Francisco: HarperCollins, 2000), pp. 170–172. This work provides a detailed history of this often elusive religion and its followers. Another reference that will repay a visit is D. Michael Quinn, *Same-Sex Dynamics among Nineteenth-Century Americans: A Mormon Example* (Urbana: University of Illinois Press, 1996). Quinn, an eminent Mormon historian, presents the Mormons as once having been more inclusive of sexual dissidents, becoming more intolerant relatively recently.
32. The discussion that follows is based in Graff's brief presentation of these philosophical differences, the one she identifies as associated with "tribal and

despotic societies," and the other with "democratic egalitarianism." See Graff, *What Is Marriage For?*, p. 176.

33. See the discussion of *Zablocki* and marriage as a individual right in the first chapter, and the discussion in Chapter Three of the connection between law and morality appropriate to the liberal-democratic regime of a constitutionally-ordered republic such as the United States.

Chapter Eight. "Gay Marriage" in the Courts

1. We do not take up the interesting issue of "intersexual" marriages involving transsexual men and women. The reader is recommended to consult Phyllis Randolph Frye and Alyson Dodi Meiselman, "Same-Sex Marriages Have Existed Legally in the United States for a Long Time Now," *Albany Law Review* 64 (2001), which challenges the ideal of "heterosexual, vaginal-penile" marriage from novel angles.
2. 852 P.2d 44, 51, n.11 (Hawaii 1993).
3. Accessible background information regarding the gay rights movement can be found in Barry D. Adam's classic study, *The Rise of a Gay and Lesbian Movement* (Boston: Twayne, 1987), while relevant original source materials from the 1950s and 1960s are usefully reproduced in Mark Blasius and Shane Phelan, eds., *We Are Everywhere*, Part III.
4. Recommended to the reader is the edited volume by Kathy Peiss and Christina Simmons, *Passion & Power: Sexuality in History* (Philadelphia: Temple University Press, 1989). This work covers a range of issues involving sexuality in cultural and social practice, and the chapters are written by recognized experts.
5. Goldfarb, "Family Law, Marriage, and Heterosexuality," argues that this falls on persons who do not meet the "heterosexual intercourse requirement."
6. 191 N.W. 2d 185 (1971).
7. *Id.* at 186, 187.
8. 191 N.W. 2d 185, 187 (1971).
9. *Id.* at 186.
10. Jones v. Hallahan, Ky., 501 S.W. 2d 588, 589–590 (1973).
11. *Id.* at 589, 590.
12. 501 S.W. 2d 588, 589 (1973).
13. *Id.* at 589.
14. 501 S.W. 2d 588, 590 (1973). In the discussion of *McGowan* in Chapter Five we noted that the Court acknowledged the infringement of religious freedom being asserted, only to ignore it.
15. *Id.* at 589.
16. Singer v. Hara Wash.App., 522 P.2d 1187 (1974).
17. *Id.* at 1192.
18. Wash.App., 522 P2d 1187, 1195 (1974).
19. *Id.* at 1195.
20. Adams v. Howerton, 486 F.Supp. 1119, 1122 (1980). This case also involved immigration law and state law. The decision was affirmed on appeal (673 F.2d 1036 [1982]).
21. *Id.* at 1123.

22. 486 F.Supp. 1119, 1123 (1980) (emphasis added). The *Adams* Court also elaborated the necessity of protecting the procreative relationship and the environment in which children are raised as the basis for the ban on same-sex marriage. *Id.* at 1124–1125. The goal of procreation does not require state support, and no-one should fear a slacking off in this area. In an increasing number of jurisdictions the goal of childrearing is no bar to same-sex couples adopting children, or keeping custody of their biological offspring. Public policy considerations traditionally taken to bar same-sex marriage were presented and discussed in the Introduction.
23. See Buchanan, "Same-Sex Marriage," 546, 549, 570.
24. The ban on same-sex marriage also affects believers who may happen to be gay or lesbian, who may wish to pursue a freedom of religious expression issue in addition to the establishment issue.
25. 30 L.Ed 220, 228 (1886).

Conclusion

1. *U.S. Dept. of Agriculture v. Moreno,* 413 U.S. 528, 534 (1973) (Brennan, J., Opinion of the Court) (emphasis original).
2. Hartog, *Man and Wife in America,* pp. 22, 312.
3. Hart, *Law, Liberty, and Morality,* p. 52.

Bibliography

Adam, Barry D., THE RISE OF A GAY AND LESBIAN MOVEMENT (Boston: Twayne, 1987).

Altman, Dennis, GLOBAL SEX (Chicago: University of Chicago Press, 2001).

Babst, Gordon A., JUST BECAUSE YOU'RE ACCEPTED DOESN'T MEAN YOU BELONG: AN INQUIRY INTO THE SOCIAL MEANING AND VALUE OF AMERICAN CITIZENSHIP (unpublished dissertation, 1996).

Bailey, Derrick Sherwin, HOMOSEXUALITY AND THE WESTERN CHRISTIAN TRADITION (London: Longmans, Green and Co., 1955).

Baird, Robert M., and Stuart E. Rosenbaum, eds., MORALITY AND THE LAW (Buffalo: Prometheus, 1988).

———. SAME-SEX MARRIAGE: THE MORAL AND LEGAL DEBATE (Amherst: Prometheus, 1997).

Barnett, Walter, *Corruption of Morals—The Underlying Issue of the Pornography Commission Report*, no. 2 ARIZONA STATE UNIVERSITY L. J. 189 (1971).

Barrett, Ellen M., *Legal Homophobia and the Christian Church*, 30 HASTINGS L. J. 1019 (1979).

Barry, Brian, JUSTICE AS IMPARTIALITY (Oxford: Clarendon Press, 1995).

Berg, Thomas C., THE STATE AND RELIGION. IN A NUTSHELL (St. Paul: West Group, 1998).

Bitton, Davis, and Maureen Ursenbach Beecher, eds., NEW VIEWS OF MORMON HISTORY. A COLLECTION OF ESSAYS IN HONOR OF LEONARD J. ARRINGTON (Salt Lake City: University of Utah Press, 1987).

Blackstone, William, COMMENTARIES ON THE LAWS OF ENGLAND (Chicago: Callaghan and Company, 3rd Ed. Revised 1962 [1884, orig. 1769]).

Blandin, Randall, *Baker v. Vermont: The Vermont State Supreme Court Held that Denying Same-Sex Couples the Benefits and Privileges of Marriage Is Unconstitutional*, 9 LAW & SEXUALITY 349 (1999–2000).

Blasius, Mark, GAY AND LESBIAN POLITICS: SEXUALITY AND THE EMERGENCE OF A NEW ETHIC (Philadelphia: Temple University Press, 1994).

———, and Shane Phelan, eds., WE ARE EVERYWHERE: A HISTORICAL SOURCEBOOK OF GAY AND LESBIAN POLITICS (New York: Routledge, 1997).

Blau, Joseph L., ed., CORNERSTONES OF RELIGIOUS FREEDOM IN AMERICA (New York: Harper & Row, 1964).

Boaz, David, LIBERTARIANISM: A PRIMER (New York: Free Press, 1997).

Brant, Irving, JAMES MADISON: THE NATIONALIST, 1780–1787 (Indianapolis: Bobbs-Merrill, 1948).

Breckenridge, Sophonisba, THE FAMILY AND THE STATE. SELECT DOCUMENTS (Chicago: University of Chicago Press, 1934).

Brody, David Eliot, and Arnold R. Brody, THE SCIENCE CLASS YOU WISH YOU HAD (New York: Perigree/Berkley Publishing Group, 1997).

Brumby, Edward, *What Is in a Name: Why the European Same-sex Partnership Acts Create a Valid Marital Relationship*, 28 GEORGIA J. OF INTERNATIONAL AND COMPARATIVE L. 145 (1999).

Buchanan, G. Sidney, *Same-Sex Marriage: The Linchpin Issue*, 10 UNIVERSITY OF DAYTON L. REV. 541 (1985).

Burns, J. H., ed., THE CAMBRIDGE HISTORY OF POLITICAL THOUGHT 1450–1700 (Cambridge: Cambridge University Press, 1991).

Butler, Judith, GENDER TROUBLE: FEMINISM AND THE SUBVERSION OF IDENTITY (New York: Routledge, 1990).

Chambers, David L., *What If? The Legal Consequences of Marriage and the Legal Needs of Lesbian and Gay Male Couples*, 95 MICHIGAN L. REV. 447 (1996).

Chapman, John W., and Alan Wertheimer, eds., NOMOS XXXII. MAJORITIES AND MINORITIES (New York: New York University Press, 1990).

Chesler, Robert Douglas, *Imagery of Community, Ideology of Authority: The Moral Reasoning of Chief Justice Burger*, 18 HARVARD CIVIL RIGHTS–CIVIL LIBERTIES L. REV. 457 (1983).

Clarkson, Kevin G., David Orgon Coolidge, and William C. Duncan, *The Alaska Marriage Amendment: The People's Choice on the Last Frontier*, 16 ALASKA L. REV. 213 (1999).

Cranor, Carl F., *Legal Moralism Reconsidered*, 89 ETHICS 147 (1979).

Cruz, David B., *"Just Don't Call It Marriage": The First Amendment and Marriage as an Expressive Resource*, 74 SOUTHERN CALIFORNIA L. REV. 925 (2001).

Curry, Thomas J., THE FIRST FREEDOMS: CHURCH AND STATE IN AMERICA TO THE PASSAGE OF THE FIRST AMENDMENT (New York: Oxford University Press, 1986).

Dent, George, Jr., *The Defense of Traditional Marriage*, 15 J. OF L. & POLITICS 581 (1999).

Dizard, Jan E., and Howard Gadlin, THE MINIMAL FAMILY (Amherst: University of Massachusetts Press, 1990).

Dreisbach, Daniel L., *The Constitution's Forgotten Religious Clause: Reflections on the Article VI Religious Test Ban*, 38 J. OF CHURCH AND STATE 261 (1996).

Drinan, Robert F., *The Loving Decision and the Freedom to Marry*, 29 OHIO STATE L. J. 358 (1968).

Duncan, Richard F., *From Loving to Romer: Homosexual Marriage and Moral Discernment*, 12 BRIGHAM YOUNG UNIVERSITY J. OF PUBLIC L. 239 (1998).

Dworkin, Ronald, *Lord Devlin and the Enforcement of Morals*, 75 YALE L. J. 986 (1966).

Dynes, Wayne K., and Stephen Donaldson, eds., HOMOSEXUALITY: DISCRIMINATION, CRIMINOLOGY, AND THE LAW (New York: Garland, 1992).

Eck, Diana L., A NEW RELIGIOUS AMERICA: HOW A "CHRISTIAN COUNTRY" HAS BECOME THE WORLD'S MOST RELIGIOUSLY DIVERSE NATION (San Francisco: HarperCollins, 2001).

Eskridge, William N., Jr., THE CASE FOR SAME-SEX MARRIAGE: FROM SEXUAL LIBERTY TO CIVILIZED COMMITMENT (New York: Free Press, 1996).

———. *No Promo Homo: The Sedimentation of Antigay Discourse and the Channeling Effect of Judicial Review*, 75 NEW YORK UNIVERSITY L. REV. 1327 (2000).

Feinberg, Joel, SOCIAL PHILOSOPHY (Englewood Cliffs: Prentice-Hall, 1973).

———. *Legal Moralism and Freefloating Evils*, 61 PACIFIC PHILOSOPHICAL QUARTERLY 122 (1980).

Feldman, Stephen M., PLEASE DON'T WISH ME A MERRY CHRISTMAS: A CRITICAL HSITORY OF THE SEPARATION OF CHURCH AND STATE (New York: New York University Press, 1997).

Foster, Henry H., Jr., *Marriage: A Basic Civil Right of Man*, 37 FORDHAM L. REV. 51 (1968–69).

Frank, Daniel H., ed., COMMANDMENT AND COMMUNITY: NEW ESSAYS IN JEWISH LEGAL AND POLITICAL PHILOSOPHY (Albany: State University of New York Press, 1995).

Frye, Phyllis Randolph, and Aylson Dodi Meiselman, *Same-Sex Marriages Have Existed Legally in the United States for a Long Time Now*, 64 ALBANY L. REV. 1031 (2001).

Gallagher, John, *Marriage, Hawaiian Style*, 726 ADVOCATE 22 (1997).

Gaus, Gerald F., JUSTIFICATORY LIBERALISM: AN ESSAY ON EPISTEMOLOGY AND POLITICAL THEORY (Oxford: Oxford University Press, 1996).

Gedicks, Frederick Mark, THE RHETORIC OF CHURCH AND STATE: A CRITICAL ANALYSIS OF RELIGION CLAUSE JURISPRUDENCE (Durham: Duke University Press, 1995).

Goldfarb, Sally, *Family Law, Marriage, and Heterosexuality: Questioning the Assumptions*, 7 TEMPLE POLITICAL & CIVIL RIGHTS L. REV. 285 (1998).

Goldstein, Anne B., *History, Homosexuality, and Political Values: Searching for the Hidden Determinants of* Bowers v. Hardwick, 97 YALE L. J. 1073 (1988).

Gonsiorek, John C., and James D. Weinrich, eds., HOMOSEXUALITY: RESEARCH IMPLICATIONS FOR PUBLIC POLICY (Newbury Park: SAGE, 1991).

Goody, Jack, THE DEVELOPMENT OF THE FAMILY AND MARRIAGE IN EUROPE (Cambridge: Cambridge University Press, 1983).

Gordon, Daniel R., *The Ugly Mirror:* Bowers, Plessy *and the Reemergence of the Constitutionalism of Social Stratification and Historical Reinforcement*, 19 J. OF CONTEMPORARY L. 21 (1993).

Gordon, Sarah Barringer, *"Our National Hearthstone": Anti-Polygamy Fiction and the Sentimental Campaign Against Moral Diversity in Antebellum America*, 8 YALE J. OF L. AND HUMANITIES 295 (1996).

Gottfried, Adele Eskeles, and Allen W. Gottfried, eds., REDEFINING FAMILIES: IMPLICATIONS FOR CHILDREN'S DEVELOPMENT (New York: Plenum Press, 1994).
Gottlieb, Stephen E., MORALITY IMPOSED: THE REHNQUIST COURT AND LIBERTY IN AMERICA (New York: New York University Press, 2000).
Graff, E. J., WHAT IS MARRIAGE FOR? THE STRANGE SOCIAL HISTORY OF OUR MOST INTIMATE INSTITUTION (Boston: Beacon Press, 1999).
Green, Steven K., *Justice David Josiah Brewster and the "Christian Nation" Maxim*, 63 ALBANY L. REV. 427 (1999).
Gusfield, Joseph R., *On Legislating Morals: The Symbolic Process of Designating Deviance*, 56 CALIFORNIA L. REV. 54 (1968).
Halley, Janet E., *Reasoning About Sodomy: Act and Identity In and After* Bowers v. Hardwick, 79 VIRGINIA L. REV. 1721 (1993).
Hammond, Phillip E., WITH LIBERTY FOR ALL: FREEDOM OF RELIGION IN THE UNITED STATES (Louisville: Westminster John Knox Press, 1998).
Hardy, B. Carmon, SOLEMN COVENANT: THE MORMON POLYGAMOUS PASSAGE (Urbana: University of Illinois Press, 1992).
Hart, H. L. A., LAW, LIBERTY, AND MORALITY (Stanford: Stanford University Press, 1963).
Hartman, Keith, CONGREGATIONS IN CONFLICT: THE BATTLE OVER HOMOSEXUALITY (New Brunswick: Rutgers University Press, 1996).
Hartog, Hendrik, MAN AND WIFE IN AMERICA: A HISTORY (Cambridge: Harvard University Press, 2000).
Harvard Law Review, *Recent Legislation*, 114 HARVARD L. REV. 1421 (2001).
Helminiak, Daniel A., WHAT THE BIBLE REALLY SAYS ABOUT HOMOSEXUALITY (Tajique, New Mexico: Alamo Square Press, 2000).
Henkin, Louis, *Morals and the Constitution: The Sin of Obscenity*, 63 COLUMBIA L. REV. 391 (1963).
Herek, Gregory M., *Myths About Sexual Orientation: A Lawyer's Guide to Social Science Research*, 1 L. & SEXUALITY 133 (1991).
Herman, Didi, RIGHTS OF PASSAGE: STRUGGLES FOR LESBIAN & GAY EQUALITY (Toronto: University of Toronto Press, 1994).
Herman, Jordan, *The Fusion of Gay Rights and Feminism: Gender Identity and Marriage After* Baehr v. Lewin, 56 OHIO STATE L. J. 985 (1995).
Hertzberg, Arthur, The Protestant "Establishment," Catholic Dogma, & the Presidency, 30 COMMENTARY 277 (1960).
Hill, Marvin S., QUEST FOR REFUGE: THE MORMON FLIGHT FROM AMERICAN PLURALISM (Salt Lake City: Signature Books, 1989).
Hill, Marvin S., and James B. Allen, eds., MORMONISM AND AMERICAN CULTURE (New York: Harper & Row, 1972).
Hillman, Eugene, POLYGAMY RECONSIDERED: AFRICAN PLURAL MARRIAGE AND THE CHRISTIAN CHURCHES (Maryknoll, New York: Orbis Books, 1975).
Hunter, Nan D., *Life After* Hardwick, 27 HARVARD CIVIL RIGHTS-CIVIL LIBERTIES L. REV. 531 (1992).
Ingram, John Dwight, *A Constitutional Critique of Restrictions on the Right to*

Marry—Why Can't Fred Marry George—Or Mary and Alice at the Same Time?, 10 J. OF CONTEMPORARY L. 33 (1984).
Jordan, Mark D., THE INVENTION OF SODOMY IN CHRISTIAN THEOLOGY (Chicago: University of Chicago Press, 1997).
———. THE SILENCE OF SODOM: HOMOSEXUALITY IN MODERN CATHOLICISM (Chicago: University of Chicago Press, 2000).
Jung, Patricia Beattie, and Ralph F. Smith, HETEROSEXISM: AN ETHICAL CHALLENGE (Albany: State University of New York Press, 1993).
Kadish, Sanford H., *The Crisis of Overcriminalization*, 374 ANNALS OF THE AMERICAN ACADEMY OF POLITICAL AND SOCIAL SCIENCE 157 (1967).
Karst, Kenneth L., *The Freedom of Intimate Association*, 89 YALE L. J. 624 (1980).
———. BELONGING TO AMERICA: EQUAL CITIZENSHIP AND THE CONSTITUTION (New Haven: Yale University Press, 1989).
Katz, Jonathan Ned, THE INVENTION OF HETEROSEXUALITY (New York: Dutton/Penguin, 1995).
Katz, Pamela S., *The Case for Legal Recognition of Same-Sex Marriage*, 8 J. OF L. & POLICY 61 (1999).
Keller, Christopher J., *Divining the Priest: A Case Comment on* Baehr v. Lewin, 12 L. & INEQUALITY 483 (1994).
Kilbride, Philip L., PLURAL MARRIAGE FOR OUR TIMES: A REINVENTED OPTION? (Westport, Connecticut: Bergin & Garvey, 1994).
King, Andrew J., *Sunday Law in the Nineteenth Century*, 64 ALBANY L. REV. 675 (2000).
Konvitz, Milton R., *Separation of Church and State: The First Freedom*, 14 L. AND CONTEMPORARY PROBLEMS 44 (1949).
Koppelman, Andrew, *The Miscegenation Analogy: Sodomy Law as Sex Discrimination*, 98 YALE L. J. 145 (1988).
———. ANTIDISCRIMINATION LAW AND SOCIAL EQUALITY (New Haven: Yale University Press, 1996).
Kramnick, Isaac, and R. Laurence Moore, THE GODLESS CONSTITUTION: THE CASE AGAINST RELIGIOUS CORRECTNESS (New York: W. W. Norton, 1996).
Krause, Harry D., FAMILY LAW. IN A NUTSHELL (St. Paul: West Publishing Co., 3rd ed. 1993).
Kurdek, Lawrence A., and J. Partrick Schmitt, *Relationship Quality of Partners in Heterosexual Married, Heterosexual Cohabiting, and Gay and Lesbian Relationships*, 51 J. OF PERSONALITY AND SOCIAL PSYCHOLOGY 711 (1986).
Laycock, Douglas, *"Nonpreferential" Aid to Religion: A False Claim about Original Intent*, 27 WILLIAM AND MARY L. REV. 875 (1986).
Layman, Gregory, THE GREAT DIVIDE: RELIGIOUS AND CULTURAL CONFLICT IN AMERICAN PARTY POLITICS (New York: Columbia University Press, 2001).
Leahy, Michael, and Dan Cohn-Sherbok, eds., THE LIBERATION DEBATES: RIGHTS AT ISSUE (London: Routledge, 1996).
Leslie, Christopher R., *Creating Criminals: The Injuries Inflicted by "Unenforced" Sodomy Laws*, 35 HARVARD CIVIL RIGHTS–CIVIL LIBERTIES L. REV. 103 (2000).

Levy, Leonard W., CONSTITUTIONAL OPINIONS: ASPECTS OF THE BILL OF RIGHTS (New York: Oxford University Press, 1986).

———. ORIGINAL INTENT AND THE FRAMERS' CONSTITUTION (New York: Macmillan, 1988).

———. THE ESTABLISHMENT CLAUSE: RELIGION AND THE FIRST AMENDMENT (Chapel Hill: University of North Carolina Press, 2nd ed., revised 1994).

Lewis, Claudia A., *From This Day Forward: A Feminine Moral Discourse on Homosexual Marriage,* 97 YALE L. J. 1783 (1988).

Louch, A. R., *Sins and Crimes,* 43 PHILOSOPHY 38 (1968).

Marshall, William P., *The Other Side of Religion,* 44 HASTINGS L. J. 843 (1993).

May, Geoffrey, MARRIAGE LAWS AND DECISIONS IN THE UNITED STATES. A MANUAL (New York: Russell Sage Foundation, 1929).

McKenzie, David, *The Supreme Court, Fundamentalist Logic, and the Term "Religion,"* 33 J. OF CHURCH AND STATE 731 (1991).

Mendus, Susan, ed., JUSTIFYING TOLERATION: CONCEPTUAL AND HISTORICAL PERSPECTIVES (Cambridge: Cambridge University Press, 1988).

Meyers, Diana Tietjens, et al., eds., KINDRED MATTERS: RETHINKING THE PHILOSOPHY OF THE FAMILY (Ithaca: Cornell University Press, 1993).

Michaelson, Sherryle E., *Religion and Morality Legislation: A Reexamination of Establishment Clause Analysis,* 59 NEW YORK UNIVERSITY L. REV. 301 (1984).

Mill, John Stuart, ON LIBERTY (New York: Prometheus, 1986 [orig. 1859]).

Monsma, Stephen V., and J. Christopher Soper, eds., EQUAL TREATMENT OF RELIGION IN A PLURALISTIC SOCIETY (Grand Rapids: William B. Eerdmans, 1998).

Moran, Rachel F., INTERRACIAL INTIMACY: THE REGULATION OF RACE & ROMANCE (Chicago: University of Chicago Press, 2001).

Nahmod, Sheldon H., *The Public Square and the Jew as Religious Other,* 44 HASTINGS L. J. 865 (1993).

Nedrow, G. Keith, *Polygamy and the Right to Marry: New Life for an Old Lifestyle,* 11 MEMPHIS STATE UNIVERSITY L. REV. 303 (1981).

Nicholas, Jack, THE GAY AGENDA: TALKING BACK TO THE FUNDAMENTALISTS (Amherst: Prometheus Books, 1996).

Nolan, Laurence C., *The Meaning of* Loving: *Marriage, Due Process and Equal Protection(1967–1990) as Equality and Marriage, from* Loving *to* Zablocki, 41 HOWARD L. J. 245 (1998).

Noll, Mark A., *The Constitution at 200: Should Christians Join the Celebration?,* 31 CHRISTIANITY TODAY 18 (1987).

Note, *In Sickness and in Health, in Hawaii and Where Else?: Conflict of Laws and Recognition of Same-Sex Marriages,* 109 HARVARD L. REV. 2038 (1996).

Note, *The Legality of Homosexual Marriage,* 82 YALE L. J. 573 (1973).

Ostling, Richard N., and Joan K. Ostling, MORMON AMERICA: THE POWER AND THE PROMISE (San Francisco: HarperCollins, 2000).

Otto, Rudolf, THE IDEA OF THE HOLY: AN INQUIRY INTO THE NON-RATIONAL FACTOR IN THE IDEA OF THE DIVINE AND ITS RELATION TO THE RATIONAL, John W. Harvey, trans. (London: Oxford University Press, 1958).

Patterson, Charlotte J., *Children of Lesbian and Gay Parents*, 63 CHILD DEVELOPMENT 1025 (1992).

Patterson, Nicholas J., *The Repercussions in the European Union of the Netherlands' Same-Sex Marriage Law*, 2 CHICAGO J. OF INTERNATIONAL L. 301 (2001).

Peddicord, Richard, GAY AND LESBIAN RIGHTS. A QUESTION: SEXUAL ETHICS OR SOCIAL JUSTICE? (Kansas City: Sheed & Ward, 1996).

Peiss, Kathy, and Christina Simmons, eds., PASSION & POWER: SEXUALITY IN HISTORY (Philadelphia: Temple University Press, 1989).

Penas, Dwight J., *Bless the Tie That Binds: A Puritan-Covenant Case for Same-Sex Marriage*, 8 L. & INEQUALITY 533 (1990).

Pennock, J. Roland, and John W. Chapman, eds., NOMOS XXX. RELIGION, MORALITY, AND THE LAW (New York: New York University Press, 1988).

Perry, Michael J., *Substantive Due Process Revisited: Reflections On (And Beyond) Recent Cases*, 71 NORTHWESTERN UNIVERSITY L. REV. 417 (1976).

———. THE CONSTITUTION, THE COURTS, AND HUMAN RIGHTS (New Haven: Yale University Press, 1982).

Plamenatz, John, MAN AND SOCIETY: A CRITICAL EXAMINATION OF SOME IMPORTANT SOCIAL AND POLITICAL THEORIES FROM MACHIAVELLI TO MARX (London: Longman's, 1963).

Posner, Richard A., SEX AND REASON (Cambridge: Harvard University Press, 1992).

Prager, Dennis, *Homosexuality, the Bible, and Us—a Jewish Perspective*, no. 112 PUBLIC INTEREST 60 (1993).

Primoratz, Igor, ETHICS AND SEX (London: Routledge, 1999).

Quinn, D. Michael, SAME-SEX DYNAMICS AMONG NINETEENTH-CENTURY AMERICANS: A MORMON EXAMPLE (Urbana: University of Illinios Press, 1996).

Rawls, John, POLITICAL LIBERALISM (New York: Columbia University Press, 1993).

———. COLLECTED PAPERS, Samuel Freeman, ed. (Cambridge: Harvard University Press, 1999).

Regan, Milton C., Jr., FAMILY LAW AND THE PURSUIT OF INTIMACY (New York: New York University Press, 1993).

Richards, David A.J., *Sexual Autonomy and the Constitutional Right to Privacy: A Case Study in Human Rights and the Unwritten Constitution*, 30 HASTINGS L. J. 957 (1979).

———. *Sexual Preference as a Suspect (Religious) Classification: An Alternative Perspective on the Unconstitutionality of Anti-Lesbian/Gay Initiatives*, 55 OHIO STATE L. J. 491 (1994).

———. WOMEN, GAYS, AND THE CONSTITUTION: THE GROUNDS FOR FEMINISM AND GAY RIGHTS IN CULTURE AND LAW (Chicago: University of Chicago Press, 1998).

Richardson, Diane, ed., THEORISING HETEROSEXUALITY: TELLING IT STRAIGHT (Buckingham, England: Open University Press, 1996).

Rorty, Richard, *Religion as Conversation-Stopper*, 3 COMMON KNOWLEDGE 1 (1994).

Rubenstein, Marc L., *Gay Rights and Religion: A Doctrinal Approach to the Argument that Anti-Gay Rights Initiatives Violate the Establishment Clause*, 46 HASTINGS L. J. 1585 (1995).

Ruskay-Kidd, Scott, *The Defense of Marriage Act and the Overextension of Congressional Authority*, 97 COLUMBIA L. REV. 1435 (1997).

Sands, Kathleen M., ed., GOD FORBID: RELIGION AND SEX IN AMERICAN PUBLIC LIFE (New York: Oxford University Press, 2000).

Savin-Williams, Ritch C., and Kenneth M. Cohen. eds., THE LIVES OF LESBIANS, GAYS, AND BISEXUALS: CHILDREN TO ADULTS (Fort Worth: Harcourt Brace & Company, 1996).

Schombert, Harold P., Baehr v. Lewin: *How Far Has the Door Been Opened? Finding a State Policy for Recognizing Same-Sex Marriages*, 16 WOMEN'S RIGHTS L. REPORTER 331 (1995).

Schur, Edwin M., LABELING WOMEN DEVIANT: GENDER, STIGMA, AND SOCIAL CONTROL (New York: Random House, 1984).

Schwartz, Louis B., *Morals Offenses and the Model Penal Code*, 63 COLUMBIA L. REV. 669 (1963).

Scott, Kieran, and Michael Warren, eds., PERSPECTIVES ON MARRIAGE: A READER (New York: Oxford University Press, 2nd ed. 2001).

Sealing, Keith E., *Blood Will Tell: Scientific Racism and the Legal Prohibitions against Miscegenation*, 5 MICHIGAN J. OF RACE AND L. 559 (2000).

———. *Polygamists out of the Closet: Statutory and State Constitutional Prohibitions against Polygamy Are Unconstitutional under the Free Exercise Clause*, 17 GEORGIA STATE UNIVERSITY L. REV. 691 (2001).

Segers, Mary C., and Ted G. Jelen, A WALL OF SEPARATION?: DEBATING THE PUBLIC ROLE OF RELIGION (Lanham: Rowman & Littlefield, 1998).

Sickels, Robert J., RACE, MARRIAGE AND THE LAW (Albuquerque: University of New Mexico Press, 1972).

Silverstein, Arthur J., *Constitutional Aspects of the Homosexual's Right to a Marriage License*, 12 J. OF FAMILY L. 607 (1972–73).

Sloan, Irving J., HOMOSEXUAL CONDUCT AND THE LAW (New York: Oceana, 1987).

Specter, Arlen, *Defending the Wall: Maintaining Church/State Separation in America*, 18 HARVARD J. OF L. & PUBLIC POLICY 575 (1995).

Stein, Stuart J., *Common-Law Marriage: Its History and Certain Contemporary Problems*, 9 J. OF FAMILY L. 271 (1970).

Stevens, Jacqueline, *Leviticus in America: The Politics of Sex Crimes*, 1 J. OF POLITICAL PHILOSOPHY 105 (1993).

Stone, Lawrence, UNCERTAIN UNIONS: MARRIAGE IN ENGLAND 1660–1753 (Oxford: Oxford University Press, 1992).

Stott, John R. W., *Homosexual "Marriage": Why same-sex partnerships are not a Christian option*, 29 CHRISTIANITY TODAY 21 (1985).

Strasser, Mark, *Family, Definitions, and the Constitution: On the Miscegenation Analogy*, 25 SUFFOLK UNIVERSITY L. REV. 981 (1991).

———. *Domestic Relations Jurisprudence and the Great, Slumbering* Baehr: *On*

Bibliography 151

Definitional Preclusion, Equal Protection, and Fundamental Interests, 64 FORDHAM L. REV. 921 (1995).

Sullivan, Andrew, ed., SAME-SEX MARRIAGE: PRO AND CON. A READER (New York: Vintage Books/Random House, 1997).

Sunstein, Cass R., *Preferences and Politics*, 20 PHILOSOPHY & PUBLIC AFFAIRS 4 (1991).

———. *Homosexuality and the Constitution*, 70 INDIANA L. J. 1 (1994).

Swanson, Wayne R., THE CHRIST CHILD GOES TO COURT (Philadelphia: Temple University Press, 1990).

Tribe, Laurence H., *Contrasting Constitutional Visions: Of Real and Unreal Differences*, 22 HARVARD CIVIL RIGHTS-CIVIL LIBERTIES L. REV. 95 (1987).

University of Hawai'i Law Review, *Recent Developments—For Better or for Worse, in Sickness and in Health, Until Death Do Us Part: A Look at Same-Sex Marriage in Hawaii*, 16 UNIVERSITY OF HAWAI'I L. REV. 447 (1994).

Wallenstein, Peter, *Law and the Boundaries of Place and Race in Interracial Marriage*, 32 AKRON L. REV. 557 (1999).

Warner, Michael, FEAR OF A QUEER PLANET: QUEER POLITICS AND SOCIAL THEORY (Minneapolis: University of Minnesota Press, 1993).

Wenz, Peter S., ABORTION RIGHTS AS RELIGIOUS FREEDOM (Philadelphia: Temple University (Press, 1992).

Weyrauch, Walter O., and Sanford N. Katz, AMERICAN FAMILY LAW IN TRANSITION (Washington: Bureau of National Affairs, Inc., 1983).

Wilkinson III, J. Harvie, and G. Edward White, *Constitutional Protection for Personal Lifestyles*, 62 CORNELL L. REV. 563 (1977).

Wolinsky, Marc, and Kenneth Sherrill, eds., GAYS AND THE MILITARY: JOSEPH STEFFAN VERSUS THE UNITED STATES (Princeton: Princeton University Press, 1993).

Wood, Forrest G., THE ARROGANCE OF FAITH: CHRISTIANITY & RACE IN AMERICAN FROM THE COLONIAL ERA TO THE TWENTIETH CENTURY (Boston: Northeastern University Press, 1990).

Wood, James E., Jr., *"No Religious Test Shall Ever Be Required": Reflections on the Bicentennial of the U.S. Constitution*, 29 J. OF CHURCH AND STATE 199 (1987).

Woods, Karen M., *Law Making: A "Wicked and Mischievous Connection": The Origins of Indian-White Miscegenation Law*, 23 LEGAL STUDIES FORUM 37 (1999).

Yarbrough, Tinsley E., *Church, State, and the Rehnquist Court: A Brief for Lemon*, 38 J. OF CHURCH AND STATE 59 (1996).

Young, Gary L., Jr., *The Price of Public Endorsement: A Reply to Mr. Marcosson*, 64 UMKC L. REV. 99 (1995).

Young, Kimball, ISN'T ONE WIFE ENOUGH? (New York: Henry Holt, 1954).

Index

Adams v. Howerton, 486 F.Supp. 103, 104, 105
Amendment Two (Colorado), 45
Anti-gay initiatives, legislation, or statutes, 8, 53–55

Baehr v. Lewin, 20, 24, 100–101
Baker v. Nelson, 102, 103
Ban on same-sex marriage, ix, x, 1, 2, 4, 5, 10, 47, 49, 52, 54, 56, 58, 65, 66, 78, 87, 88, 89, 91, 94, 98–99, 102, 105, 107, 108, 109, 110
Barr, Robert, 28
Barry, Brian, 52
Blackstone, William, 41, 42, 45, 46, 48, 51
Board of Education v. Barnette, 37
Boaz, David, 18, 83
Bowers v. Hardwick, 6, 42
Bradwell v. Illinois, 87
Brause v. Bureau of Vital Statistics, 24
Buchanan, Sidney, 46, 104–105

Child adoption, custody, or rearing, 8, 9, 25, 26, 103
Cleveland Bd. Of Educ. v. LaFleur, 16
Coats, Dan, 28

Davis v. Beason, 96, 97
Defense of Marriage Act (DOMA), 5, 10, 21, 22–33, 101, 107
Devlin, Patrick, 42–45, 46, 48, 51, 110
Due Process, 15, 16, 27, 31
Duncan, Richard, 93–94

Dworkin, Ronald, 44

Equal protection, 3, 15, 27, 89, 91
Equal rights, equality, 9, 23, 25, 31, 49, 57, 59, 83, 110
Everson v. Board of Education, 67, 71, 73

Faction, religious faction, 47, 50, 55
Family, family forms, 9, 101
Federalism, 27
Federalist No. 10, 47
Feldman, Stephen, 64
First Amendment, 3, 5, 52, 54, 56, 64, 77–79, 83, 96, 105, 107–108, 110
Fourteenth Amendment, 3, 15–16, 27, 31
Freedom of conscience, liberty of conscience, 33, 51, 52, 56–58, 78, 83, 108
Freedom of religion, religious freedom, ix, 32, 39, 51–53, 58, 108
Full Faith and Credit Clause, 7, 26
Fundamental right(-s), ix, 3, 15, 23–24, 27, 31, 49, 58, 65–66, 79, 108

Gaus, Gerald, 47
Gay marriage, 3, 4–5, 100–105
Gay or lesbian parents, 8, 9
Gay persons, 1, 8, 20, 51, 52, 55–56, 65–66, 82, 98, 99, 108, 110
Gay rights, 7–8
Gender, gender norms, 7, 9–10, 24–25
Griswold v. Connecticut, 15

Hart, H.L.A., 42–44, 110
Hartog, Hendrik, 109
Helms, Jesse, 29
Hertzberg, Arthur, 64
Heteroexclusivity, 19, 27, 103, 110
Heteronormativity, 4, 20, 28, 31, 33, 39, 57, 82, 94, 98
Heterosexism, 20, 39, 94
Heterosexual or opposite-sex couples, 9, 18–19, 24, 25–26, 39, 56, 82
Heterosexuality, 19–20
Hobbes, Thomas, 47
Homosexuality, homosexuals, 20, 38, 39, 42, 45, 52, 53, 54, 65, 82, 99

Interracial marriage, mixed-race couples, ix, 4, 13, 18, 28, 32, 65, 91–94

Jelen, Ted, 47
Jones v. Hallahan, Ky., 102–103
Jordan, Mark, 41

Karst, Kenneth, 15, 38
Keller, Christopher, 57
Koppelman, Andrew, 92
Krause, Harry, 19

Layman, Gregory, 32
Levy, Leonard, 58
Libertarianism, 18, 83–84
Liberty interest(-s), ix, 3–4, 14, 15, 23, 27, 31, 33, 49–50, 57, 58, 59, 65, 74, 98, 108
Locke, John, 51
Loving v. Virginia, 13, 15, 24, 92, 93, 94, 103

Madison, James, 47, 69, 78
Marriage, argument from definition, 5, 24, 66, 80–84, 102, 103, 104
Marriage, as civil contract, 16–18, 22, 107
Marriage, as civil status, 18–20, 105, 107
Marriage, as fundamental right, ix, 15, 58, 65, 105. *Also see:* fundamental right(-s)
Marriage, as protected liberty interest, ix, 15, 58, 65, 105. *Also see:* liberty interest(-s)
Marriage, as voluntary, personal decision, 17, 18, 98
Maynard v. Hill, 13–14
McCollum v. Board of Education, 67–73, 78
McGowan v. Maryland, 67, 72–78, 94, 104, 105
McLaughlin v. Florida, 92
Mill, John Stuart, 38, 97
Miscegenation, anti-miscegenation laws, 5, 66, 88, 91–94
Mormonism, Mormons, ix, 4, 5, 89, 95–99
Murphy v. Ramsey, 96

No religious test clause, ix, 3, 63–65
Non-preferentialism, 57, 64, 68, 70, 71, 78
Nussbaum, Martha, 38

Paine, Thomas, 51
Perez v. Lippold, 92, 103
Plural marriage, polygamy, anti-polygamy laws, 19, 66, 88, 95–99
Privacy right, 15, 24
Procreation, 25–26
Public, as contrasted with secular, 2
Public law, policy, or purpose, 2, 3–4, 6–10, 22, 25, 27, 30, 33, 57–58, 64, 73, 78–79, 82–83, 88, 100, 107, 108–109, 111

Regan, Milton, 19
Religion, 1–2
Reynolds v. United States, 95, 96, 103
Richards, David A.J., 48, 51–59, 71, 83, 92, 107–108
Romer v. Evans, 8

Same-sex couples, 8, 9, 18, 24–26, 82, 98, 108
Sectarian, defined, 2
Sexual orientation, 7–9, 20, 24, 30, 42, 58, 82, 94, 101
Shadow Establishment, *sub rosa* religious establishment, ix, 1–5, 10, 28,

44, 53, 57–58, 65–66, 67–79, 80–81, 83–84, 95–97, 100, 105, 108, 110
Shelley, Martha, 55–56
Singer v. Hara Wash.App., 103
Skinner v. Oklahoma, 16
Smith, Rogers, 33
Sodomy, anti-sodomy laws, 6–7, 41, 65, 101–102, 109
Solemnizing of marriage, 17, 83
Stan Baker, et al. v. State of Vermont, et al., 25
Stevens, Jacqueline, 82
Sunday closing laws, ix, 4–5, 67, 72–78, 100

Sunstein, Cass, 27, 91

Tenth Amendment, 16
Tolerance, toleration, 51, 52
Torasco v. Watkins, 64–65

Wolfenden Report, 43

Yick Wo v. Hopkins, 105

Zablocki v. Redhail, 15, 16, 18
Zorach v. Clauson, 67, 69–72, 77, 78

Teaching Texts in Law and Politics

David Schultz, *General Editor*

The new series Teaching Texts in Law and Politics is devoted to textbooks that explore the multidimensional and multidisciplinary areas of law and politics. Special emphasis will be given to textbooks written for the undergraduate classroom. Subject matters to be addressed in this series include, but will not be limited to: constitutional law; civil rights and liberties issues; law, race, gender, and gender orientation studies; law and ethics; women and the law; judicial behavior and decision-making; legal theory; comparative legal systems; criminal justice; courts and the political process; and other topics on the law and the political process that would be of interest to undergraduate curriculum and education. Submission of single-author and collaborative studies, as well as collections of essays are invited.

Authors wishing to have works considered for this series should contact:
>Peter Lang Publishing
>Acquisitions Department
>275 Seventh Avenue, 28th floor
>New York, New York 10001

To order other books in this series, please contact our Customer Service Department at:
>800-770-LANG (within the U.S.)
>(212) 647-7706 (outside the U.S.)
>(212) 647-7707 FAX

or browse online by series at:
>WWW.PETERLANGUSA.COM